Latino-American History

The Spanish Conquest of America

Prehistory–1775

Latino-American History

The Spanish Conquest of America
Prehistory to 1775

Independence for Latino America
1776–1821

Spanish Settlement in North America
1822–1898

Struggling to Become American
1899–1940

Fighting for American Values
1941–1985

Creating a New Future
1986 to Present

Latino-American History

The Spanish Conquest of America

Prehistory–1775

by Michael Burgan

Mark Overmyer-Velázquez, Ph.D., Consulting Editor

CHELSEA HOUSE PUBLISHERS
An imprint of Infobase Publishing

COVER *In 1540, Francisco Vásquez de Coronado explores what will one day be the U.S. Southwest.*

The Spanish Conquest of America

Copyright ©2007 by Infobase Publishing

For information contact:

Chelsea House
An imprint of Infobase Publishing
132 West 31st Street
New York, NY 10001

Library of Congress Cataloging-in-Publication Data
Burgan, Michael.
    The Spanish conquest of America / Michael Burgan.
        p. cm. — (Latino American history)
    Includes bibliographical references and index.
    ISBN 0-8160-6440-7 (hardcover)
    1. America—Discovery and exploration—Spanish—Juvenile literature. 2. Southwest, New—Discovery and exploration—Spanish—Juvenile literature. 3. Spain—Colonies—America—History—Juvenile literature. 4. Southwest, New—History,—to 1848—Juvenile literature. I. Title. II. Series.
    E123B87 2006
    979'.01—dc222006017145

Cover design by Takeshi Takehashi

A Creative Media Applications Production
Interior design: Fabia Wargin & Luis Leon
Editor: Matt Levine
Copy editor: Laurie Lieb

Photo Credits
The Granger Collection, New York, pages: cover, 12, 34, 37, 40, 46, 54, 72, 88, 92; North Wind Picture Archives pages: vi, 22, 50, 58, 63, 67, 78, 95; Library of Congress pages: 8, 20, 52; Biblioteca Medicea-Laurenziana, Florence, Italy/The Bridgeman Art Library page: 16; Service Historique de la Marine, Vincennes, France, Lauros/Giraudon/The Bridgeman Art Library pages: 19, 71; New York Public Library, Astor, Lenox and Tilden Foundations pages: 26, 29, 43; Peter Newark American Pictures/The Bridgeman Art Library page: 68; The Bridgeman Art Library page: 85

Maps: Created by Ortelius Design

Printed in the United States of America

Bang Pkg ____ ____ 10 9 8 7 6 5 4 3 2 1

This book is printed on acid-free paper.

All links and Web addresses were checked and verified to be correct at the time of publication. Because of the dynamic nature of the Web, some addresses and links may have changed since publication and may no longer be valid.

Contents

Preface to the Series

**by Mark Overmyer-Velázquez, Ph.D.,
Consulting Editor**

"With all due respect to Uncle Sam, this [march] shows that Los Angeles has never stopped belonging to Mexico." This statement by Alberto Tinoco, a television reporter in Mexico, refers to the demonstration in support of immigrants that took place in Los Angeles, California, on March 25, 2006. An estimated 1 million people attended this march—mainly Mexicans and other Latinos. But does Los Angeles belong to Mexico? And what was so important that so many people came out to show their support for Latino immigrants?

The *Latino American History* series looks to answer these questions and many others. Los Angeles did belong to Mexico until 1848. At that time, Los Angeles and much of what is now called the American Southwest became part of the United States as a result of the Mexican-American War. Today, the enormous city, like many other places throughout the United States, is home to millions of Latinos.

The immigrant march made perfectly clear that people of Latin American descent have a historical power and presence in the United States. Latino history is central to

OPPOSITE Bartolome de las Casas, a Spanish priest who defended American Indian rights, tries to protect the Aztecs from the Spanish.

the history of the United States. Latinos have been closely connected to most regions in the United States in every era, from the 16th-century Spanish settlements in Florida and California to the contemporary surge of Latino populations in North Carolina, South Carolina, Oklahoma, Minnesota, and Connecticut.

The 2000 U.S. Census made Latinos' importance even plainer. Every 10 years, the government makes a survey of the country's population, called a census. The 2000 survey determined that, for the first time, Latinos outnumbered African Americans as the second-largest nonwhite population.

One of every seven people in the nation identifies himself or herself as Latino. This ethnic group has accounted for about half the growth in the U.S. population since 1990. There are over 41 million people of Latin American and Caribbean origins in the United States. Their presence will have a large impact on the futures of both the United States and Latin America.

Who Is Latino?

The term *Latino* emerged in the 1970s. It refers—somewhat loosely—to people, either male or female, living in the United States who have at least one parent of Latin American descent. The term is often used in contrast to terms such as *Anglo American, African American,* and *Asian American.* Most frequently, *Latino* refers to immigrants (and their descendants) who originally came to the United States from the Spanish-speaking countries of North, Central, and South America, as well as from countries in the

Caribbean. This definition usually does not include Brazil, Haiti, and Belize, where the chief language is not Spanish, but does include Puerto Rico, which is a U.S. territory.

The other popular term to describe this population, *Hispanic,* was developed by the U.S. government in the 1970s as a way to categorize people of Latin American descent. However, Latinos consider this label to wrongly identify them more with Spain than with Latin America. In addition, most Latinos first identify with their own national or subnational (state, city, or village) origins. For example, a woman with roots in the Dominican Republic might first identify herself as *una dominicana* and then as a Latina. The word *Latino* causes further confusion when discussing the thousands of non–Spanish-speaking American Indians who have immigrated to the United States from Latin America.

Four main factors over time have determined the presence of Latinos in the United States. They are U.S. military and economic involvement in Latin America, relaxed immigration laws for entry into the United States, population growth in Latin America, and wages that were higher in the United States than in Latin America. These factors have shaped the patterns of migration to the United States since the mid-19th century.

"We Didn't Cross the Border, the Border Crossed Us"   1848

Many Mexicans still call the Mexican-American War from 1846 to 1848 the "North American Invasion." In the first decades of the 19th century, Mexico's economy and military were weak from years of fighting. There had been a war for independence from Spain followed by a series of civil wars among its own people. During the same period, the United States was eager to expand its borders. It looked to Mexico for new land. The war cost Mexico almost half its territory, including what would become the U.S. states of California, Nevada, Arizona, New Mexico, and Texas. Some Mexican citizens left on the U.S. side of the new border proclaimed, "We didn't cross the border, the border crossed us."

The territory that had belonged to Mexico brought new citizens of Mexican background to the United States, as well as enormous mineral and land wealth. Consider the famous gold rush that started in 1848 on former Mexican territory in California. That event and the vast expanse of farmlands and pasture lands once belonging to Mexico were vital to the westward expansion of the United States. Mexicans on the north side of the new border became U.S. citizens and the country's first Latinos. As the West became industrialized and demand for labor grew, it was often migrant Mexican workers who labored in the fields and factories of the prospering economy.

1898   The Spanish-American War, Puerto Rico, and the Harvest of Empire

The term *harvest of empire* refers to the arrival of Latino immigrants in the United States as a direct result of U.S. military involvement in Latin America, starting with Mexico in 1848. The United States created political and economic uncertainty through the use of force and the support of dictatorships in the "garden" of Latin America. Then the United States harvested the resulting millions of homeless and jobless Latinos. The United States's harvest of empire peaked with the 1898 Spanish-American War.

The U.S. military freed the island of Puerto Rico from Spanish colonial rule in 1898. The island's residents never would have imagined that they would be colonized yet again, this time by the United States. The island became a U.S. territory. The U.S. president had the power to choose the governor and other high-level administrators. In 1917, Congress made all Puerto Ricans U.S. citizens.

In the 1950s, Puerto Rico suffered economic problems and joblessness. Immigration to the United States rapidly expanded, resulting in the largest movement of Latin Americans to the United States in history. New laws in the 1960s only increased Latin American immigration to the United States.

> **Fast Fact**
>
> American Indians who have migrated to the United States may identify themselves with a small village or perhaps a state of origin. For example, Zapoteco immigrants from the state of Oaxaca, Mexico, have developed Oaxacan hometown associations in Los Angeles and other U.S. cities.

The Hart-Celler Act and Recent Latino Migration

1965

On October 3, 1965, President Lyndon Johnson signed the Hart-Celler Act, introducing a new era of mass immigration. The act made people's work skills and their need to unite with their families the most important elements in deciding who could immigrate to the United States. The new legislation eventually ended a system that used people's countries of origin to decide the number of immigrants who were allowed into the United States. The Hart-Celler Act supposedly put people of all nations on an equal footing to immigrate to the United States. The act created the foundation for today's immigration laws.

Between 1960 and 2000, Latin America's population skyrocketed from 218 million to over 520 million. Political instability in the region, in addition to this growing population, meant increased needs for migration and work. Many people turned to the economic opportunities of the United States as a strategy for survival.

At the same time, in the United States, agricultural, industrial, and domestic employers depended upon the ability to pay immigrant laborers from Latin America lower wages. As a result, Latino labor has almost always been welcomed in the United States, despite the government's repeated attempts to restrict immigration in the past century. The demands of U.S. employers for Latino immigrant labor have always shaped the tone of the immigration debate.

> **Fast Fact**
>
> In 1960, 75 percent of the foreign-born population of the United States came from Europe. Only 14 percent came from Latin America and Asia. As a result of the Hart-Celler Act, by 2000, only 15 percent of immigrants were European and more than 77 percent were Latin American and Asian. This trend promises to continue.

Many Latino Histories

The events of the years 1848, 1898, and 1965 explain how and why Latinos migrated to the United States. However, these events do not reveal much about what happened once the Latinos arrived. Despite their many shared experiences, Latinos are anything but an easily defined people. Although television and film have tended to portray all Latinos as similar, they come from a wide range of national, ethnic, social, economic, and political backgrounds, which have divided as much as united this growing population. Such backgrounds include "African," "Anglo," "Asian," "Indian," and any combinations of these.

Mexicans started migrating to the United States in the 19th century and Puerto Ricans in the early 20th century. Immigrants from Chile, Argentina, El Salvador, Guatemala, and other South and Central American countries made their way north in large numbers starting in the 1960s. Many of these Latinos were seeking shelter from brutal military dictatorships. Once in the United States, Latinos of all backgrounds have continued to mix with each other and with local populations, forging a whole new set of identities. Latino communities keep and develop their own cultures in new and creative ways in the United States, adding to the rich diversity of the country.

Indeed, Latinos have contributed to U.S. society in other ways besides their investments in the country's economy and labor. In politics, education, sports, and the arts, Latinos are a growing presence. By exploring the origins and development of U.S. Latinos, this series, *Latino American History*, helps us to better understand how our Latin American neighbors to the south have become our Latino neighbors next door.

Introduction

In 1469, Queen Isabella of Castile married Aragon's King Ferdinand. Their wedding united two kingdoms in Iberia, the region of western Europe that now comprises Spain and Portugal. Soon, Spain would begin to build one of the largest empires the world has ever seen.

Colonies in the New World

Twenty-three years after Ferdinand and Isabella's marriage united Spain, an Italian sailor named Christopher Columbus sailed on a voyage of discovery with the backing of the Spanish monarchs. Columbus believed he could sail west from Europe and reach Asia. On that first voyage in 1492 and three more that followed, Columbus never came close to Asia. Yet he and his crew did go ashore in the West Indies and Central and South America. Columbus had stumbled across two continents unknown to Europeans of the time. They called these lands "the New World."

As Columbus made his discoveries, he claimed the lands he found for Spain. Thinking he had reached the East Indies, islands off the coast of Southeast Asia, he used the term *Indians* for the native peoples that he met. By using this

OPPOSITE In 1493, after his return from the New World, Christopher Columbus presents American Indians to King Ferdinand and Queen Isabella of Spain.

general term, the Spaniards lost sight of the fact that individual tribes of American Indians were not all the same—they had different languages and cultures.

Columbus started the first Spanish colonies in the West Indies. Using American Indians and then Africans as slaves, the Spaniards mined gold and other valuable minerals. Soon, farming became the main source of income. The slaves raised sugarcane that produced great profits in the markets of Europe.

A Desire to Expand

Ferdinand and Isabella had various reasons for supporting Columbus and building colonies in the New World. Aragon had a tradition of trading overseas, sending its textiles to other parts of Europe and the Middle East. In the hunt for overseas trade and wealth, Spain competed against the other major European powers of the day. With Columbus's first voyage, Ferdinand and Isabella hoped to open up a new trade route to the East Indies and perhaps also tap into the wealth believed to exist in China and Japan. Once they realized they had reached a new part of the world, the Americas, the Spaniards wanted to shut out their European competitors. The Spaniards hoped to keep the region's natural resources to themselves, especially after they discovered silver in Peru and Mexico. In the centuries to come, Spain battled various European rivals for control of its new empire.

Many Spaniards had another reason for seeking new lands to rule—they wanted to spread their religious faith. To Europeans of that time, religion was an important part of daily life. The government and the church usually worked together to keep order in society. At times, however, they competed for power, and both patterns continued in the Americas. The Spanish government sent missionaries to convert the Native Americans, but the missionaries and local political officials often clashed on how to run the colonies.

The Push to the North

In the 16th century, the Spaniards moved beyond their colonies in the West Indies. The first major target was Mexico, which became the heart of a colony known as New Spain. They also moved farther north. During the rest of the 16th century, the Spaniards explored the southern part of what became the United States, and they founded colonies in present-day Florida and New Mexico.

The early explorers and settlers of these colonies confronted native tribes who fought skillfully and bravely against the invading Spaniards. A small number of Spaniards—as well as other Europeans and African slaves—settled in the Spanish lands of North America, and missionaries there continued to try to convert the American Indians. Europeans, Indians, and Africans together built the Spanish colonies in what became the United States.

By the time of the American Revolution (1775–1783), Spain had settlers in the Southwest, California, Louisiana, and Florida. Less than a century later, all those lands would be under U.S. control. Yet the influence of Spanish culture in those regions remains strong, shaping modern Latino influence in the United States.

The First Americans

1

Long before Christopher Columbus ever dreamed of sailing across the ocean, people lived throughout the Americas. Starting more than 13,000 years ago and perhaps even much earlier, groups of people from northeast Asia began coming to the Americas. Most likely, they either walked across a strip of land that once linked Asia and Alaska or sailed to the west coast of North America. From their first landing points, these Asian settlers spread out across North and South America, a process that took several thousand years.

The earliest American Indians survived by hunting, fishing, and gathering nuts, seeds, and wild fruit. About 10,000 years ago, some tribes in Central and South America began domesticating wild crops. They took the seeds from wild plants to raise food for themselves. These first farmers settled in one spot to raise crops, creating villages, rather than roaming from one hunting ground to another. A similar development of agriculture and towns had already taken place in parts of western Asia.

By A.D. 1000, several great civilizations had developed in the Americas, such as the Beni in South America. High in

OPPOSITE Christopher Columbus is depicted departing from Spain on his 1492 journey in this colored engraving from 1594.

New Theories on the First Americans

For several decades, most historians accepted the theory that ancestors of today's American Indians came from northern Asia and spread southward from Alaska. In recent years, however, some scientists have suggested that some of the first Americans may have originally come from Africa or Australia. Human skulls more than 8,000 years old have been found in Brazil. They are similar in shape and size to the skulls of modern Africans and to Australian native people. One scientist suggests that ancient people with roots in Africa may have crossed from Asia to Alaska long before the northern Asian migrants did. Others ponder whether the first settlers might have sailed directly from Africa.

the Andes Mountains, the Beni built towns around Bolivia's Lake Titicaca. Several hundred years after the rise of the Beni, the neighboring Inca of Peru created the greatest civilization in the Americas. The Inca built thousands of miles of roads to connect the distant parts of their empire. They also built huge stone palaces and used knotted cords to keep records of business deals and other important information.

The Maya lived in Central America in A.D. 1000. They built large, stepped pyramids for their dead kings—monuments that still survive today. The Maya also developed a 365-day calendar based on the movement of the sun. The Toltec, northern neighbors of the Maya, were later replaced by a group of three American Indian peoples who are commonly called the Aztec today.

Farther north, the Anasazi lived in what is now the U.S. Southwest. They were influenced by two nearby peoples with similar lifestyles, the Mogollon and Hohokam. The Anasazi used irrigation to grow crops in a harsh desert environment. The Anasazi also built large adobe buildings similar to modern apartments that housed hundreds of people. In what became the U.S. Midwest and Southeast, people known today as the Mississippians built huge mounds to bury their kings. At its peak, their largest city, Cahokia, had a population of at least 10,000. Some of the great Indian cities further south, in Mexico and South America, were ten times as big.

American Indians in Spanish Lands

When Christopher Columbus came ashore in the Bahamas on October 12, 1492, at least several million people—and perhaps as many as 25 million—lived across the Americas. The first native people he met were the Arawak of the West Indies, who included a distinct group called the Taino. These people gave Columbus and his crew a warm welcome. Like American Indians on the mainland, the Taino and other Arawak raised such crops as corn, beans, and squash, along with manioc, a root vegetable. They also fished, sometimes using nets made from cotton, which they also raised. The islands lacked large wild animals, so hunting was limited to small mammals and reptiles.

Although the Arawak had not created huge cities, they did have thriving kingdoms ruled by a leader called a cacique. Religion was an important part of life for all American Indians, and the Arawak worshipped many different gods. They often honored their gods with dances and festivals.

Fast Fact

The wild plants that American Indians domesticated included maize, which is commonly called corn in the United States. Maize was most likely developed from a wild mountain grass called teosinte. This grass had tiny ears with just a dozen or so kernels on each.

This 16th-century illustration by Spaniard Bernardino de Sahagun shows Aztecs viewing a map and then following it.

Central Mexico in 1492 was dominated by the Aztec. Of the three peoples who created the Aztec culture, the Mexica were the most important. According to their myths, in 1325, an eagle guided them to the spot where they founded their capital, Tenochtitlán (modern-day Mexico City.) Seeing the spot, the Mexica supposedly said, "Oh happy, oh blessed are we! We have beheld the city that shall be ours." Over the next 100 years, the Mexica and their allies built a huge city with a population of 250,000. Tenochtitlán had temples and other massive public buildings, and its citizens farmed and fished. Some became traders, selling goods brought from hundreds of miles away. The Aztec were skilled warriors, and they soon defeated rival tribes and created a great empire.

Tribes of the Southwest and Florida

To the north of Mexico, the Anasazi civilization had faded by 1492, but it left behind pockets of people who still followed the old ways. They took water from nearby rivers to raise their crops, and they lived in adobe houses, though not as big as the largest Anasazi buildings. Some also lived in homes built inside caves in the mountains of the Southwest. Today's Hopi, Zuni, and Pueblo Indians are the descendants of the Anasazi. In the years before Columbus's arrival, they raised corn, squash, and beans and made baskets and pottery. Some also worked in turquoise, a stone found throughout the region.

New tribes also pushed into the Southwest from the north. The Navajo and Apache came down from Canada and the western plains. When the Spanish reached the region, they converted the Navajo from nomads into settled farmers. The Apache, however, remained mostly hunters, using horses (introduced to the New World by the Spanish) to seek their game—and occasionally to raid other Indian villages.

Outdoor Fun

Many American Indians played games that used balls. The Taino and other Arawak built large courts, called *bateys,* for their ball game. Both men and women played this game, which was similar to soccer. Players moved the ball with almost every part of the body except their hands. The ball was made from rubber and cotton and could be dangerous if it struck a player at high speeds. Players often wore padding and stone belts to protect themselves. The Taino and Arawak ball games were usually part of larger celebrations attended by different communities. The remains of the ball courts have been found on several islands of the West Indies.

Along the east coast of North America, the Indians of Florida enjoyed a friendlier climate. The southern end of the peninsula was inhabited by the Tequesta and Calusa. They did not grow many crops, instead relying on fish and shellfish for much of their food. The Tequesta also hunted alligators and whales and made a kind of flour from the root of a local plant, the zamia. The Calusa rounded out their diet with wild fruit and small mammals.

The Calusa dominated southern Florida from their capital city of Calos. This city and other Calusa towns were built along the coast on huge mounds of seashells. The Calusa also built canals so their boats could move goods and people across the region. The largest Calusa boats were long canoes with sails, able to carry 50 people.

When Spain built its first missions and forts in Florida, most were located in the north, along the Atlantic coast and into the interior. (A mission was a settlement where Christianity was preached for the first time in an area where there were no native priests.) The major tribes there were the Apalachee and the Timucua. This region had forests and good soil for growing crops. The Timucua in particular cut down and burned trees and other growth to prepare fields for farming.

The Apalachee had the largest villages in northern Florida. They traced their roots to the earlier Mississippians, and their capital near Lake Jackson had seven large mounds. The capital was the home of the main chief, while subchiefs ruled neighboring communities. These lower chiefs came to the capital at different times to honor the main chief, bringing gifts of corn and animal skins, including bear and rabbit.

American Indians of Florida paddle a dugout canoe past their village in this engraving from 1591.

Into the Southeast

By 1492, the Apalachee were not the only descendants of the Mississippians in North America. Traces of the earlier mound-building culture were found in tribes throughout what became the southeastern United States. Some of these tribes, which the Spaniards later met, were the Coosa, Cherokee, Mobile, Choctaw, and Chickasaw. They stretched out over an area that included modern-day Tennessee, Kentucky, Alabama, Georgia, Mississippi, and Missouri.

The last of the mound-builders were the Natchez, who lived along the lower Mississippi River. Their ruler, called the Great Sun, lived on a mound, as did other important figures in the tribe. Common farmers and laborers lived in huts that ringed the mounds. The people grew a variety of crops, including tobacco, which was used in religious ceremonies.

Tribes of the West Coast

Far from the Mississippi River, along the Pacific Ocean, a different American Indian culture developed. What became the state of California was home to about 300,000 people by the time Columbus sailed. They spoke more than 80 different languages and were divided into what historians call "tribelets"—small groups of perhaps 50 people.

Mound-builders such as these could be found throughout what would become the southeastern United States when Europeans first arrived in the Americas.

The American Indians of California did not farm. Like the Calusa of Florida, they relied on the ocean for most of their food. They also gathered a wide assortment of wild foods that grew in California's moderate climate. These included hazelnuts, plums, and especially acorns. The people ground acorns and used them to make soup and bread.

The tribes of California included the Chumash, whose skilled workers created carvings out of soapstone, worked with wood, and made beads. Junípero Serra, the Spanish missionary who helped Spain settle California, noted that the Chumash had "pleasing ways and engaging manners." Farther south were the Ipai and Tipai, the first tribes Serra encountered when he entered California from Mexico in 1769. Today, they are known collectively as the Kumeyaay Nation. Villagers moved together from winter to summer sites chosen for their nearness to water and supplies of acorns.

No matter where they lived, the Indians of North America believed that a variety of spirits lived in nature and that some humans with special powers, called shamans, could contact them. Most tribes also thought that people could not own land; they merely took what nature provided, while doing as little damage as possible to the forests and streams. The Spaniards who came to North America thought that Christianity was the one true religion and that the Indians' religions defied God's teachings. Since the Indians lacked the true faith, the Spaniards believed that it was morally acceptable for them to enslave the Indians and take over land that their ancestors had lived on for centuries. Relations with the first Americans shaped Spain's attempts to control North America, often with deadly results for both sides. ▣

The Spanish Arrive

2

About 2,000 years ago, at the time of the Roman Empire, most of Europe was part of a vast international trade network that stretched from Africa to Asia. When the Roman Empire collapsed, its former lands in Europe were cut off from much of that trade. Over the next centuries, European merchants slowly began to reach out to the world again. Italians played a key role in this trade. Merchants in the cities of Venice and Genoa set up trading posts in cities located along the Black and Crimean Seas. There, they dealt with Arab merchants who brought spices and other goods from Asia.

In the 13th century, Marco Polo of Venice made a remarkable trading voyage that took him to China. A book about his travels described a wealthy nation ruled by a leader called the Great Khan. Polo wrote that this man lived in a palace that was "the most extensive that has ever yet been known." The Great Khan had vast supplies of silver, gold, gems, and pearls, and he traded with lands rich in such spices as pepper, nutmeg, and cinnamon. These spices did not grow in Europe, so their use was seen as a sign of great wealth.

OPPOSITE Marco Polo's ships are shown leaving Venice to visit China in this 14th-century illustration. Polo's voyage raised other Europeans' interest in expanding trade.

A Discovery before Columbus

For centuries after Columbus's voyage of 1492, people thought that he was the first European to reach the Americas and leave a trace of his visit. About 1000, however, Leif Eriksson sailed from his home in Greenland and reached a land he called Vinland. He and his crew put up several buildings and met native people they called *skraelings*. Almost 1,000 years later, a Norwegian scientist named Helge Ingstad proved that items he found in Newfoundland, Canada, had belonged to Eriksson and his crew. Today, Eriksson is honored as the first European to reach North America, while Columbus is credited with establishing the first permanent contact between the Old World and the New.

Portugal Leads the Way

After Polo's trip, Europeans were eager to expand their trade with Asia. By land, the route was long and dangerous, because the Muslims of central Asia often attacked Christians who tried to pass through their countries. At last, in the 15th century, Europeans turned to the sea as the best way to reach India, China, and the other lands of the Far East. At that time, the Portuguese perfected a new ship design. Borrowing from the Arabs, they built ships called caravels. The sails made it easy to travel in all kinds of wind conditions, and caravels were easier to steer than other ships. The Portuguese also improved their navigational skills and created naval charts that detailed coastlines and wind conditions in certain areas.

Portugal had a ruler eager to expand his country's trade and win converts to Christianity. Prince Henry was often called Henry the Navigator because of his interest in ships and ocean travel. He was curious about the world beyond Europe. Under his rule, Portugal began Europe's first major program of overseas exploration and trade. Starting in 1433, Portuguese ships began to sail farther south along the coast of Africa, and by 1442, they had landed on the continent to trade for slaves and gold. A Portuguese ship reached the southern tip of Africa in 1488. Soon, the Portuguese would round the continent and head for India.

Columbus Sails West

Born in the Italian seaport of Genoa, Christopher Columbus was exposed to the sea and ships from an early age. He began his career at sea about 1465, when he was a teenager. He studied navigation and made at least one voyage to Africa on a Portuguese ship. According to his son Fernando, Columbus "began to [think] that if the Portuguese could sail so far south, it should be possible to sail as far westward, and that it was logical to expect to find land in that direction." Readings in history and geography convinced Columbus that the lands he would find were China, Japan, and the East Indies.

In 1484, Columbus approached King John II of Portugal, seeking money to make this westward journey to Asia. John turned him down, and so did King Ferdinand and Queen Isabella of Spain. At the time, they were too focused on fighting the Moors to fund a risky expedition. In 1492, after their victory over the Moors, they finally agreed to pay for Columbus's trip. They hoped to spread Christianity in Asia. Royal advisers also pointed out that Spain might gain vast new wealth from gold and spices. Ferdinand and Isabella agreed to give Columbus the title of admiral and make him viceroy of the lands he found. The viceroy was the king's representative and answered only to the king. Columbus would also receive 10 percent of any riches he discovered.

After months of preparation, Columbus sailed from Spain on August 3, 1492. His fleet consisted of two caravels, the *Niña* and the *Pinta,* and a larger, older ship called the *Santa Maria.* During the voyage, the sailors grumbled as they sailed for weeks without seeing any sign of land. On October 10, Columbus wrote that "the men lost all patience, and complained of the length of the voyage, but the Admiral encouraged them in the best manner he could." Finally, on October 12, the three ships reached land.

In the months that followed, Columbus and his crew visited several islands of the Bahamas, as well as Cuba and Puerto Rico. Columbus used the term *Indians* for the Arawak he met, thinking he had reached the East Indies of

Christopher Columbus's expedition leaves Spain on its way to the New World.

Asia. The Arawak brought Columbus small pieces of gold, which he saved to show Ferdinand and Isabella. The admiral also captured several Indians to take back to Spain.

During the trip, the *Santa Maria* ran aground on an island Columbus named Española (now called Hispaniola). The wreck of the ship, Columbus wrote, was the work of God: "Our Lord had caused me to run aground at this place so I might establish a settlement here." Columbus left behind several sailors, who built a small fort at a site Columbus called La Navidad. This became the first Spanish colony in the New World.

Spanish Settlement

After a triumphant return to Spain, Columbus prepared a second voyage. This time, he commanded 17 ships and more than 1,000 settlers. Columbus had dazzled Ferdinand and Isabella with tales of the spices and gold that waited in the Indies. In reality, however, the settlers on Hispaniola faced a difficult time. They did not find gold or

Sharing across the Ocean

The Spaniards brought many items with them from Europe to the Americas. In return, the Spaniards and the Europeans who followed them discovered new things there that they took back to Europe. This giving and taking of goods between the two parts of the world is sometimes called the Columbian exchange. The goods the Europeans introduced to the Americas included livestock, such as sheep, cattle, and goats; crops such as wheat, rice, bananas, sugar and coffee; and manufactured goods made from iron, such as pots and guns. In return, the Europeans took back such crops as corn, potatoes, tomatoes, squash, hot peppers, tobacco, and peanuts. From the American Indians, the Spaniards also learned new words, and some of them have been adapted into English. *Barbecue, hammock, hurricane, iguana,* and *tobacco* are some English words that have Arawak and Carib Indian roots.

spices, and they survived only because the native people gave them food. Although the Arawak welcomed the Spanish at first, by 1495 the Indians were rebelling against the harsh rule of the Spaniards, who had taken Arawak lands and women. Eventually, the Spaniards forced many of the Arawak into slavery.

Through the rest of the 1490s, Columbus tried to lure settlers to Hispaniola. He said that the island "abounds in everything, especially bread and meat," and that each Spaniard had "two or three Indians to serve him." But few Spaniards wanted to make a dangerous ocean crossing to live in a dangerous land so far from home. Many settlers who did make the trip died from disease, lack of food, and battles with the Arawak. For a time, Ferdinand and Isabella thought of sending prisoners to the New World, since so few people wanted to go there.

The slave labor of the Indians helped keep the settlers alive. The slaves also mined the small amount of gold found on Hispaniola. But the Arawak soon began dying of diseases, such as smallpox and measles, that the Spaniards had brought with them. The Arawak had never been exposed to these diseases before, so their bodies lacked natural defenses against them. In 1502, as the shortage of workers grew, Spain brought the first Africans to the New World. They had been born into slavery in Spain or Portugal, where slavery had existed for many years. Later, the slaves sent to the New World came directly from Africa. They raised sugarcane, which became the most important crop in the Spanish islands of the Caribbean. Later, coffee became another key crop in the West Indies.

Despite the difficulties of life on Hispaniola, the Spanish government continued to send ships west across the Atlantic Ocean. Columbus led two of these expeditions. He and other Spanish crews explored the coastline of Central and South America. By 1511, the Spanish had colonies in Puerto Rico, Cuba, and Colombia, and before the end of the decade, they also had a settlement in Panama, on the Pacific Ocean.

Hispaniola and Cuba served as the starting point for many new expeditions, and in 1518, Hernán Cortés left Cuba with almost 1,000 men to explore Mexico. Cortés had one thing on his mind. He said, "I come, not to cultivate the soil like a laborer, but to find gold." Military men such as Cortés, who led expeditions of conquest for Spain, were called conquistadores. Most were religious knights who believed that the Spanish people were chosen by God to convert the American Indians and rule over them.

Hernán Cortés (left) is pictured entering Mexico with his men in 1519.

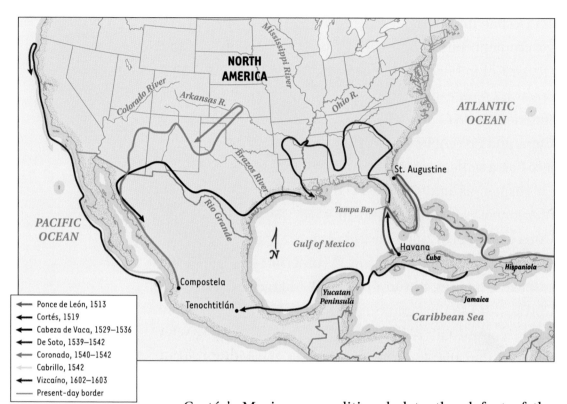

Key:
- Ponce de León, 1513
- Cortés, 1519
- Cabeza de Vaca, 1529–1536
- De Soto, 1539–1542
- Coronado, 1540–1542
- Cabrillo, 1542
- Vizcaíno, 1602–1603
- Present-day border

This map shows the progression of Spanish exploration in North America. The voyages of several prominent explorers are highlighted.

Cortés's Mexican expedition led to the defeat of the great Aztec empire in 1521. The Spaniards soon called the Aztec's lands New Spain. Millions of native people, Aztecs and members of other tribes, were now under Spanish rule. Ruling people of different ethnic and religious backgrounds was not new for the Spaniards. During the Reconquista, they had gained power over the Moors and Jews of Spain. The Spanish had also already brought slaves from Africa to Spain.

Although the Spanish ruled firmly in their new colonies, their laws protected some rights of the slaves and non-Spaniards. For example, slaves in Spanish lands could take their owners to court if they were mistreated. Additionally, the Spanish accepted marriages between themselves and

American Indians more readily than other Europeans did. Many people of mixed Mexican-Indian and Spanish heritage later settled in what became the United States.

In New Spain, the conquistadores and wealthy settlers were given control over groups of Indians and the lands they had traditionally farmed. Under this system, called *encomienda,* the Indians were not slaves, but the Spaniards received goods and services from them. In return, the Spanish "lords" were supposed to protect the Indians and help them become good Christians.

Exploring Florida

Even before Cortés led the Spanish conquest of Mexico, in March 1513, Juan Ponce de León led an expedition from Puerto Rico that came ashore on what he thought was a large island. Instead, he and his crew had landed on the mainland of what would become the United States. Ponce de León named the land *Florida,* Spanish for "flowers," because of the many flowers the Spaniards found there, and also to honor *Pascua Florida,* a Spanish term for the Easter season.

The Spaniards landed somewhere near present-day Daytona Beach. They spent the next several months exploring the coast. Ponce de León and his men sailed south, through the Florida Keys, and then northward toward what is now Fort Myers.

Fast Fact

Throughout their colonial rule in North America, Spaniards used the term La Florida to describe a large part of the southeastern United States, not just the area that became the state of Florida. La Florida stretched from the Mississippi River to the Chesapeake Bay.

Juan Ponce de León

Before he set off for Florida, Juan Ponce de León (1460–1521), already had many years of experience exploring the New World. Born in San Tervás de Campos, Spain, he sailed with Christopher Columbus on his second voyage across the Atlantic. In 1502, Ponce de León returned to Hispaniola before setting off to start the first Spanish colony in Borinquen, now known as Puerto Rico. Tales of a so-called fountain of youth may have lured him to explore farther north of that island. There is no written proof that he actually thought the fountain existed, but some historians suggest that his route to Florida may have been influenced by the legends he had heard. More likely, Ponce de León hoped to find gold and duplicate the wealth he had earned as a landowner in Puerto Rico.

Along the way, the Spaniards met the Tequesta and Calusa Indians. Ponce de León spent several weeks in Calusa territory, but fled when a fleet of 80 Calusa war canoes closed in on his three ships. He returned to Puerto Rico in September, then went to Spain, where he was greeted as a hero for claiming new lands for the empire.

In the years that followed, several Spanish sea captains charted the waters of the Gulf of Mexico. In 1519, Alonso Álvarez de Pineda sailed from Jamaica with four ships and explored the coastline of the gulf from Florida to Mexico. On his voyage, Álvarez de Pineda saw the mouth of the Mississippi River and realized that Florida was a peninsula, not an island, as Ponce de León had thought. Ponce de León, however, still had doubts, and in 1521, he set off on a second expedition. As he wrote to Spain's ruler, Charles V, the explorer wanted "to see whether [Florida] is an island, or whether it connects with the land [of New Spain]."

Ponce de León also hoped to start a colony in Florida, so he took settlers and livestock with him on his second trip. The Spaniards came ashore on the west coast, in the land of the Calusa. The settlers barely had time to build temporary shelters before the Calusa attacked. Ponce de León was hit by an arrow during the battle, and he later died from his wounds. Despite the failure of his mission, Spain would continue to explore and try to start colonies north of Mexico.

The Search for Riches

3

Around the time of Ponce de León's second Florida expedition, other Spaniards were eyeing lands farther north along the Atlantic coast. As Columbus had shown, the New World had at least one resource besides gold and spices that Europeans wanted—slaves. In 1521, a Spanish ship landed in what is now South Carolina, and its captain forced 60 Guale Indians into slavery. Some Spaniards realized that enslaved American Indians were the most valuable resource in parts of North America. The labor that the Indians provided allowed the Spanish colonies to survive.

The enslaving of the Guale Indians upset Lucas Vázquez de Ayllón, a judge in the Spanish colony on Hispaniola. Ayllón had sent the captain to explore and trade, not capture Indians. The judge arranged for the release of the Guale, but not before some of the slaves mentioned a place called Chicora. This site, somewhere in the interior of the Carolinas, was said to be rich with minerals. That tale fueled Spanish, French, and English interest in the region around South Carolina throughout the 16th century.

OPPOSITE The Moorish slave Esteban, who survived the failed expedition of Pánfilo de Narváez in the 1520s, aided the Spanish in their exploration of Arizona in 1539.

In 1526, Ayllón led an expedition to start a colony in South Carolina. Like Ponce de León before him, Ayllón sailed with livestock, supplies, and soldiers. The Spaniards landed near the mouth of the Pee Dee River and founded the village of San Miguel de Gualdape. Ayllón hoped to convert Indians, as well as build settlements in the region. Ayllón had mostly peaceful relations with the Guale—at first. Yet over several months, the colonists and the Indians battled, and the Spaniards ran out of food. As starvation and disease spread through the colony, Ayllón and hundreds of others died. The survivors returned to Hispaniola.

The Narváez Expedition

Despite Ponce de León's and Ayllón's failed attempts at colonizing, the Spanish government was not ready to give up on La Florida. Spanish officials saw that the region had a larger importance to Spain's New World empire. Controlling the Gulf of Mexico and the sailing routes of the Caribbean Sea would make it easier to protect Spanish ships in the region. King Charles V chose a brutal conquistador named Pánfilo de Narváez to start a colony on the northwest coast of the Gulf of Mexico in order to strengthen ties between New Spain and La Florida.

Under the contract between Charles and Narváez, the conquistador was expected to build three forts and convert the natives. To start his colony, he sailed from Spain in 1527 with 600 people, including 10 women, African slaves, and several priests. The expedition made stops in Hispaniola and Cuba, where some of the would-be settlers changed their minds and left the ships. Two ships were also destroyed by hurricanes. When Narváez finally reached Florida in 1528, he had just 400 people.

With Narváez on this expedition was Álvar Núñez Cabeza de Vaca. His journal describes the many hardships the settlers faced getting to Florida and after they landed. Once on shore, Narváez made a costly decision. He split up the expedition, taking most of the men on a land route to find gold and sending his ships to look for a harbor. Narváez and the men he took with him never again saw the ships, which failed to find a harbor and returned to the West Indies.

The surviving members of Pánfilo de Narváez's expedition are shown reaching the Gulf of Mexico in 1528 after having walked across Florida.

Africans in North America

The settlers on Lucas Vázquez de Ayllón's expedition to South Carolina included about 100 African slaves. They were the first Africans to live in what became the United States. Some historians believe that some of the slaves may have rebelled against the Spaniards during the difficult times at San Miguel de Gualdape. Whether they rebelled or not, some of the Africans did remain behind when the Spanish left the colony. The former slaves then lived with the American Indians of the region.

On his quest for gold, Narváez often angered the Timucua and other Native Americans he encountered. Narváez forced some of the Indians to serve as guides and translators for the expedition and he demanded food from tribal villages. Several times, the Indians attacked the Spaniards. Cabeza de Vaca wrote that on one occasion, "a number of Indians assailed us from behind trees that concealed them from our sight, while others were on fallen trees, and they began to shower arrows upon us, so that many men and horses were wounded."

After months of wandering, Narváez and his men reached the northwestern tip of Florida. Narváez ordered the men to build rafts, on which they tried to reach Spanish settlements in New Spain. However, Indians attacked the tiny vessels, and some of the rafts sank. Only four men were known to survive the failed mission of Pánfilo de Narváez; one was Cabeza de Vaca. He came ashore in Texas and then spent five years living with tribes in the present-day U.S. Southwest. Eventually, he met up with the other three survivors, and together they reached New Spain. One of the survivors, a Moorish slave named Esteban, would play a major role in a future Spanish exploration of the Southwest, leading the way into New Mexico.

Travels across La Florida

By 1537, the tale of the four survivors from Narváez's mission reached Spain. That year, a conquistador named Hernando de Soto was preparing yet another expedition to La Florida. De Soto had fought in Peru, helping to bring the great Inca empire under Spanish control. The Spanish found huge silver mines in Peru. De Soto's success there made him a wealthy man, but he sought even greater riches farther north. Charles V named de Soto *adelantado,* or governor, of La Florida, and the conquistador was determined to succeed where others had failed.

De Soto's expedition sailed from Spain to Cuba, then reached Florida in the summer of 1539. The adelantado came ashore near what is now Tampa Bay with more than 700 hundred people and 220 horses. De Soto had enough supplies for more than a year. He also planned to take food from the American Indians he met in the interior of La Florida.

De Soto led his expedition northward, toward the lands of the Apalachee. Along the way, he entered various Timucua villages. The Spaniards took food, captured women and children to serve as laborers, and threatened to kill anyone who refused their demands. Some Indians tried to fight back. One Timucua chief sent a message to de Soto: "I and all of my people have vowed to die a hundred deaths to maintain the freedom of our land." Although the Spanish had guns, armor, horses, and vicious war dogs, the Timucua knew the land. They could hide and then strike quickly, doing damage with their bows and arrows. Then they could slip back into the swamps and forests before the Spaniards could wage a counterattack.

In October 1539, de Soto reached the land of the Apalachee. He spent the winter there and then moved north into Georgia. The Spaniards pushed on through what is now the southeastern United States, meeting the descendants of the Mississippian mound builders. Local tribes showed them pearls and other valuable items, but de Soto never discovered the gold he sought. Their hunt for riches took the Spaniards westward, into present-day Mississippi, and in 1541, de Soto and his crew became the first Europeans to cross the Mississippi River.

Hernando de Soto and his men are shown during their Florida expedition of 1539 rescuing a Spanish prisoner from unfriendly American Indians.

The next year, de Soto became ill and died. The remaining explorers, about 300 of them, decided to leave La Florida. They built boats and sailed down the Mississippi into the Gulf of Mexico. Natchez Indians in canoes chased them down the river, and one called out, "If we possessed such large canoes as yours . . . we would follow you to your land and conquer it, for we too are men like yourselves."

> **Fast Fact**
>
> Hernando de Soto and other conquistadores traveled with large, ferocious dogs specially trained to attack enemies during battle. De Soto's main war dog was the greyhound.

First Trek to New Mexico

While the de Soto expedition was coming ashore at Tampa Bay in 1539, other Spaniards were already exploring the lands just north of New Spain. Several years before, when he was wandering through the Southwest, Cabeza de Vaca had heard Indians talking about seven rich cities in the mountains, known as Cíbola. These tales led Viceroy Antonio de Mendoza to send a small expedition in search of the cities. To lead this force, the viceroy chose Friar Marcos de Niza, an Italian priest who belonged to the Franciscan order. The Franciscans are one of many religious orders that are part of the Roman Catholic Church. The Moorish slave Esteban, who had survived the Narváez expedition, went along with Friar Marcos as a guide and translator.

In 1539, the expedition left New Spain and headed into what is now southern Arizona. Friar Marcos sent Esteban ahead with American Indians who were traveling with them. Soon, Esteban entered the land of the Zuni, in northwest New Mexico. The Zuni, a 16th-century Spanish historian later wrote, thought "that he must be a spy or a guide from some nations who wished to come and conquer them . . . so they decided to kill him."

The Indians traveling with Esteban returned to Friar Marcos with the news. The priest thought the Zuni city might be part of Cíbola, so he decided to see it for himself. What he saw was an adobe town, like the ones the Anasazi and their descendants had lived in for centuries. He also heard from Indians he met that the Zuni pueblo (village) was the smallest of the seven cities in the region.

When Friar Marcos returned to New Spain, he told Mendoza that the tales were true: Cíbola existed, and it had great riches. Friar Marcos lied about what he had seen, claiming that the Zuni town had "house doors studded with jewels [and] streets lined with shops of silversmiths." Historians are not sure why the priest lied. Perhaps he wanted to please the viceroy or make himself seem important.

Coronado's Quest for Riches

The priest's report excited Mendoza. He invested some of his own money in a much larger expedition to search for Cíbola. The leader of this expedition, Francisco Vásquez de Coronado, also invested heavily in the venture. More than 1,000 men, both Spaniards and American Indians, volunteered for the mission, seeking their share of the riches Coronado hoped to find. Acting as a guide was de Niza, and several other priests came along as well. Mendoza instructed Coronado to act in a "Christian" way so that "the conquest might be . . . not a butchery."

Coronado left New Spain in February 1540. After six months of crossing the desert, the expedition began to run low on food. Finally, it crossed into New Mexico and reached the Zuni pueblo of Hawikuh. Coronado was shocked by what he saw. As he wrote to Mendoza, "I can assure you that in reality [de Niza] has not told the truth in a single thing that he said . . . except the name of the city and the large stone houses."

The Zuni, however, had one thing the Spaniards needed: food. Coronado and some of his men approached the pueblo. The Zuni, frightened by the strangers and their horses, withdrew inside. As the Spaniards came closer, the Zuni fired arrows at them. Coronado's troops responded with guns and quickly won the battle. Seeing the military might of the invaders, neighboring villagers came out to make peace with the Spaniards.

The expedition of Francisco Vásquez de Coronado left New Spain in 1540 in search of riches, but Coronado found only American Indian pueblos.

From Hawikuh, Coronado sent out small teams to search for Cíbola. He still hoped to find riches. His men returned with reports of more villages and adobe pueblos farther east and north, but no signs of silver and gems. Another team discovered a huge canyon to the west.

These Spaniards were the first Europeans to see what is now called the Grand Canyon. Another group headed toward the Great Plains, searching for an unusual animal an Indian had described—the buffalo.

The Return of the Horse

The Zuni are said to have been particularly afraid of the horses Coronado and his men rode. American Indians of the 16th century had never seen such large, domesticated animals before. Early ancestors of the modern horse had once roamed wild in North America, but they died off thousands of years ago. The Spaniards brought the horse back to the continent, and some tribes began to acquire them for their own use. Through trade and theft, horses slowly appeared across the western part of North America. On the Great Plains, horses allowed the Apache and other tribes to become highly mobile hunters and warriors.

At his winter camp near the Rio Grande, Coronado heard about another American Indian city said to be filled with riches. In Quivira, the stories went, the fish were as big as horses and the ruler ate off silver and gold plates and bowls. The search for Quivira began in the spring and took Coronado and his men into western Texas and then north into what is now Oklahoma and Kansas. Their guide was a Pawnee Indian nicknamed "the Turk," because the Spaniards thought he looked Turkish.

When the expedition reached the land called Quivira, Coronado saw that he had been lied to again. He wrote to the king that the guides "had described to me houses of stone, with many stories; and not only are they not of stone, but of straw, but the people in them are as barbarous as all those whom I have seen and passed before this." Coronado killed the Turk for lying to him and then returned to spend another winter in

New Mexico. In 1543, he returned to Mexico, where he was considered a failure for not finding great wealth.

Three years later, Spain finally came across riches to match those from Peru. Silver was discovered in New Spain. New Mexico and La Florida would now attract fewer Spaniards hoping to make a fortune, but those lands would remain important to the Spanish government as it tried to protect its resources in Mexico. ▨

The First Colony

4

In 1555, Philip II became the king of Spain. He welcomed the silver flowing into his nation from New Spain and South America. The increasing Spanish wealth caught the eyes of France and Great Britain, who had also sent ships to explore the New World. France in particular seemed prepared to start colonies in North America, and French ships began to attack the Spanish vessels carrying silver from the New World. The French also attacked Havana, the capital of Cuba, and briefly controlled the city. Philip decided he needed a thriving colony in Florida that could serve as a base for the Spanish navy. His warships would protect the cargo ships loaded with silver, and his soldiers would prevent the French or other Europeans from starting their own colonies in land that Spain claimed as its own.

In 1559, an expedition led by Tristán de Luna y Arellano sailed from New Spain, heading for the west coast of the Florida peninsula. Luna had traveled with Coronado, and many of the soldiers traveling with him had served with Hernando de Soto. Also on board Luna's 13 ships were 1,000 settlers, both Spanish and American Indian. As on the past voyages to Florida, missionaries came, hoping to create converts. Some of the settlers still dreamed of finding the legendary Chicora or other Indian towns filled with riches.

In July, Luna left some of his men and supplies at a harbor in what is now Mobile Bay, Alabama. The rest of the expedition headed for a port called Ochuse, which de Soto had discovered near the land of the Apalachee. When a hurricane struck, Luna lost almost all his ships, and many of the settlers died. To find food for the survivors, Luna decided to move farther inland. He set up a camp at Nanipacana, in what is now Alabama. The colonists ate acorns, leaves, and the roots of wild plants.

Knowing he needed more food, Luna sent some of his soldiers to find Coosa, a wealthy Creek Indian settlement that de Soto had visited. The soldiers found Coosa, but not much food, so they returned to Luna's base. He and most of the settlers had by this time gone back to Ochuse, and the soldiers soon joined them. In April 1561, the colonists at Ochuse were relieved to see ships from Spain. The ships had been ordered to take the settlers from Ochuse to the eastern coast of La Florida and a port called Santa Elena (modern-day Parris Island, South Carolina). Most of the settlers, however, got off the ships in Havana. A few continued on until bad weather turned back their ships.

Fighting the French

The French were still active along the Atlantic coast, and in late 1561, Spanish officials heard that they planned to start a colony in La Florida. The French effort was led by Jean Ribault, who landed with about 150 others near modern St. Augustine, Florida, in 1562. From there, the French moved northward and built a fort at Santa Elena, which they renamed Port Royal.

Ribault and some of his crew soon returned to France for supplies. The small group of settlers who remained at Port Royal relied on friendly Guale Indians for food. Over time, however, their supplies ran out and the settlers no longer trusted their leaders to provide for them. The colonists abandoned Port Royal and returned to France. A larger group of French settlers then arrived in La Florida. By 1564, they had built Fort Caroline, near modern-day Jacksonville, Florida.

Hearing about the first French settlement, King Philip picked Pedro Menéndez de Avilés to lead an expedition to La Florida. If he defeated the French, Menéndez would become adelantado of a Spanish colony on the east coast of Florida. The news of the second, larger French colony startled Philip, who then decided to send some of his own troops on Menéndez's mission to Florida. The king was determined to end the French threat.

Menéndez's expedition totaled more than 2,500 people, though not all his ships sailed at the same time, and not all made it to Florida. In August 1565, Menéndez came ashore south of Fort Caroline. At the same time, Jean Ribault had arrived at the French fort with reinforcements. This was the first direct confrontation between the two European rivals in what became the United States.

Fast Fact

The Menéndez expedition marked the first time that the Spanish crown sent its own troops to fight in the New World. Before this, the government had relied on volunteers or men recruited by the conquistadores.

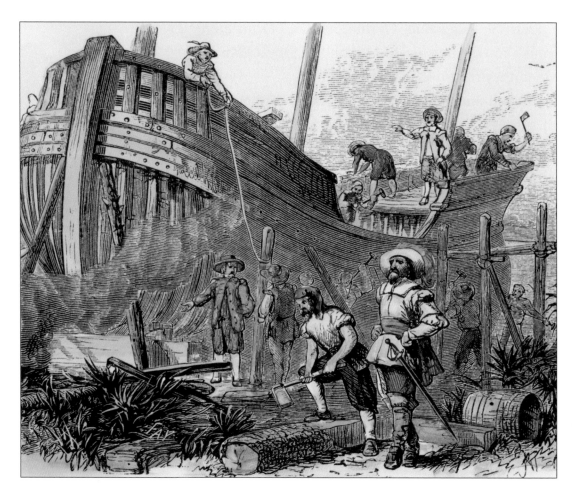

French colonists at Port Royal build a ship in 1562 while they wait for Jean Ribault to return from France with more supplies.

Menéndez took his small fleet of five ships up to Fort Caroline and fired on the French ships in the harbor. Outnumbered by the French defenders on shore, the Spanish did not land. Instead, Menéndez sailed about 40 miles (64 km) south, where his crew and some African slaves began to build their own fort on the site of a Timucua village. The settlers called their new home St. Augustine.

Ribault sailed by, saw the settlers hard at work, and decided to attack before the fort was complete. On September 10, French ships with 600 soldiers on board sailed for St. Augustine. A fierce storm blew the ships off course, and one of them was shipwrecked. About a week later, Menéndez decided to attack Fort Caroline by land. He marched 500 soldiers to the French settlement. Thanks to bad weather, the French did not see the Spanish coming. With so many of their soldiers still at sea, the French could not defend themselves. Menéndez and his men quickly took control of Fort Caroline and renamed it San Mateo. The Spanish killed more than 130 men and took several dozen women and children as prisoners.

Later in the month, Menéndez learned that the survivors of the failed French naval assault on St. Augustine were traveling by land back to Fort Caroline. They did not know about the successful Spanish attack. Menéndez took some of his men to meet the French. Seeing that they were outnumbered, the French offered to surrender if Menéndez would not kill them. Menéndez, however, showed no mercy, and all the men who were not Catholics were killed.

On October 11, another group of French survivors approached St. Augustine. Menéndez told them that France no longer controlled Fort Caroline. Some of the French decided to turn around and head south. The others, including Jean Ribault, surrendered. Once again, Menéndez slaughtered the French.

Building a Spanish Colony

With the French threat over, Menéndez could begin to build his colony. The settlers in St. Augustine included the wives and children of 26 men serving under Menéndez. Together,

Pedro Menéndez de Avilés defeated the French and drove them from Florida in 1565.

the colonists built the first permanent European settlement in what became the United States. As more ships arrived from Spain, the number of soldiers, sailors, and settlers in Florida rose to more than 2,000.

Then relations between the Spaniards in St. Augustine and the nearby Indians soured. In April 1566, Timucua warriors attacked the Spanish fort. Menéndez moved his new community to what he thought was a safer spot nearby and built a new fort. The same year, Menéndez took some of his men north and built the fort of San Salvador in Santa Elena, which was soon followed by a second fort, San Felipe. Menéndez also left a small number of troops at camps that stretched along the Florida coastline around to the western side of the peninsula. Soldiers were also stationed at San Mateo, the old Fort Caroline.

The settlers tried to grow crops as they had in Spain. Near San Felipe, they raised wheat, but floods and animals destroyed the crops. Finding enough food became a major difficulty, and some colonists seized a ship and headed to the West Indies, rather than staying in La Florida. Another group of settlers that Menéndez sent north returned to Spain when bad weather slowed their ship's progress.

In December 1566, Menéndez sent Juan Pardo on the first of two expeditions from Santa Elena into the interior.

The second began the following September. Pardo was instructed to "calm the . . . Indians of all the land and attract them to the service of God and of his majesty," the king of Spain. One goal was to find tribes who could supply the colony with food. Menéndez also wanted Pardo to scout out a route for a road that would link La Florida to New Spain. On both his trips, Pardo met Native American chiefs who promised loyalty to Spain, though they did not provide large amounts of food. Pardo also built several small forts, but since each had only a few defenders, local Indian tribes soon overran them. Pardo failed in his mission to find a road route to Mexico as well. The Spanish did not realize that the lands Pardo explored were more than 1,000 miles (1,600 km) away from New Spain.

The Missionaries

Early in 1567, the first Jesuit missionaries reached Florida. Father Juan Rogel and Brother Francisco Villareal hoped to convert the Calusa and

The Pardo Expeditions

Captain Juan Pardo arrived in St. Augustine in June 1566. He was one of 250 soldiers King Philip sent to Florida to help Menéndez defend his colony. On each of his expeditions, Pardo led about 125 men, heading northwest from Santa Elena. On the first, he explored parts of central North Carolina. On the second, he and his men reached what is now Tennessee. Pardo often wrote in his journal that the lands he saw were "very good," and he noted many Indian towns along the way. Pardo was friendly with the Indians he met, since he wanted to win their loyalty and convert them to Christianity. He gave the chiefs gifts, including axes, knives, jewelry, and cloth. Yet some of the tribes Pardo met remembered the violent ways of the soldiers under Hernando de Soto. Once Pardo returned to Santa Elena, the tribes did not waste any time destroying the forts the Spanish had built.

Tequesta of southern Florida. After fighting broke out between Spanish soldiers and both tribes, the two missionaries were forced to flee. More Jesuits arrived the next year, and some returned to southern Florida, while others tried to convert the Guale farther north. The American Indians were not open to embracing a religion practiced by people who killed them and took their food. The Jesuits tried to distance themselves from the Spanish soldiers, but Menéndez did not want the priests acting on their own.

The American Indians who labored for the missions were sometimes treated cruelly by the Spanish when the Indians did not do as the Spanish wished.

The Indians who did come to hear the missionaries teach about Christianity seemed more interested in the gifts the priests gave them. Father Rogel wrote that the Indians told him "to leave them alone; they did not want to listen to me. But by treating them with kindness and love and using handouts of corn as bribes, I was able to get them to continue coming to lessons."

One priest decided he would have more success without any soldiers nearby. In 1570, Father Juan Bautista de Segura took several other missionaries to land that the Spanish called Bahía de Santa María—modern-day Virginia. Segura wrote in September 1570 about his early meetings with the Indians of Bahía de Santa María: "We have felt the good will which this tribe is showing [and] . . . great hope is had of its conversion and of the service of Our Lord and His Majesty." Yet within one year, the Indians had turned against the Spaniards, killing all except a teenage boy who had come with them.

Children in the New World

Few single Spanish women came to La Florida, so many male settlers had children with American Indian wives. The children were called mestizos, or "mixed." The children of two Spanish parents born in the New World were called *criollos*, or creoles. They became the dominant settlers in the centuries to come, when fewer new arrivals came from Spain.

Continuing Problems

In 1572, the Jesuits decided to end their missionary efforts in La Florida. Menéndez, however, still wanted to win converts among the Indians. He had practical reasons, as

Africans in Florida

The community of Saint Augustine included both enslaved and free Africans. Some of the slaves had lived in Spain before reaching the New World. In Florida, the hardest work went to slaves who came directly from Africa or had spent some time in the West Indies. Masters, however, did not want to treat slaves too harshly, since they could easily run off and seek aid from American Indians. The Roman Catholic Church believed that Africans could become Christians, and it encouraged masters to free slaves who accepted that faith. One notable free African in early Spanish Florida was a sailor named Juanillo. In 1562, the ship on which he served was shipwrecked near Florida. He survived the wreck and spent three years living with the Timucua. Pedro Menéndez de Avilés came across Juanillo in 1565, and the African worked as a translator for the Spanish for many years.

well as religious ones. Unlike earlier conquistadores in North America, Menéndez had specific orders not to enslave the Indians. Still, he needed their labor to provide food, as his colony was struggling to survive. The forts along the southern coast had failed, and King Philip had to send money to support the troops that remained. Menéndez hoped that Indians who became Christians would help him fight enemy tribes. They would also provide the labor the Spanish needed.

Menéndez asked the Franciscans to send new missionaries, and the first arrived at the end of 1572. St. Augustine and Santa Elena were now the heart of the colony. The Franciscans went to work first near Santa Elena, converting a Guale chief. After the priests left in 1575, however, relations between the Guale and the Spanish worsened. Soldiers killed several important tribal leaders, and in 1576, the Guale and another tribe attacked the Spanish. For a time, the Spanish fled their fort at Santa Elena and sought protection in St. Augustine. Once the fort was rebuilt, the Spaniards attacked the Indians. Relations never improved. The next major attempt to convert the Indians would wait until the 17th century.

In 1586, the Spanish abandoned Santa Elena. St. Augustine became the major Spanish settlement, though its population remained small. That same year, the town came under attack. Spain and England were at war, and the English sea captain Sir Francis Drake, commanding 23 ships and 2,000 men, overpowered the Spanish and burned St. Augustine. The residents at the time included 30 African-Cuban slaves who had been brought to St. Augustine to build a new fort.

By 1600, St. Augustine had only about 500 residents. The Spanish still had not found great mineral wealth in La Florida—and never would—and relations with the American Indians remained difficult. Yet the crown wanted a Spanish presence on the peninsula, to keep out the French and English. Spain would continue to spend money on this distant colony for more than 150 years. ▣

Settling New Mexico

5

As the Spanish were trying to build their colony in Florida, some missionaries focused on lands closer to New Spain. After Coronado's expedition of the 1540s, Spain had not made any meaningful attempts to explore or colonize New Mexico. That began to change in the 1580s, when several Franciscans took steps to bring Christianity to the Pueblo Indians.

The first monk to venture northward was Agustín Rodríguez. In 1581, he organized an expedition that crossed the Rio Grande and reached the Indian villages of New Mexico. Traveling with him were two other Franciscans, some Spanish soldiers, and American Indian servants. The Spaniards went to the towns of the Zuni and Acoma Indians, and Rodríguez and another monk stayed in the region to begin their missionary work.

A second expedition, led by the Franciscan Antonio de Espejo, set off in 1582 to bring Rodríguez home. Espejo arrived to find that the two monks had been killed, but he had mostly peaceful relations with the various tribes he met. Espejo and his men traveled through parts of Arizona and Texas, as well as New Mexico. Writing about his experience,

OPPOSITE This Hopi village from the 1800s is an example of the dwellings in which the Pueblo Indians lived when the Spanish found them three centuries earlier in New Mexico and Arizona.

Espejo said he found mines "said to be by those who know very rich and to contain much silver." He also heard of gold and other riches in the region.

Espejo's report, recalling the old tales of Cíbola, stirred new interest in settling New Mexico. King Philip II was also intrigued by the many large pueblos Espejo saw. The king was determined to win new converts to the Roman Catholic Church. (In fact, the influence of the Roman Catholic Church remains strong in Latino communities in the United States today. About 75 percent of modern-day Latino Americans are Catholic.)

Fast Fact

Antonio de Espejo most likely reached what is now Prescott, Arizona. The area has some silver and gold, but it is most famous for its copper mines.

In 1583, the Spanish crown told the viceroy of New Spain, Luis de Velasco, to choose someone to start a colony in New Mexico. That process took 15 years. In the meantime, several expeditions set off for the northern lands without the viceroy's permission. The first of these illegal expeditions ended in 1591, when Spanish soldiers tracked down the would-be colonists and brought them back to New Spain. The second group managed to reach modern-day Nebraska before being killed by American Indians.

Oñate Enters New Mexico

Finally, in 1595, the viceroy of New Spain chose Juan de Oñate to lead an official expedition into New Mexico. Oñate's father had served under Hernán Cortés during the conquest of the Aztecs, and his family had made a fortune mining silver in New Spain. Over the next several years, Oñate recruited settlers, though far fewer than he wanted. The expedition that left in January 1598 numbered about 600 people, including women, children, Franciscans, and American Indians. Some of the settlers had come from Spain, while others had already spent time in the New World. The settlers traveled with livestock and carts loaded with supplies. Hopeful he would find silver, Oñate brought mining equipment.

By April 1598, the settlers reached a spot along the Rio Grande River near present-day El Paso, Texas. Oñate had the settlers build a church, and on April 30, he nailed a cross into a tree, part of the ceremony that officially made the lands he found part of Spain.

Over the next few months, the expedition moved into northern New Mexico, near the village of the San Juan Pueblo Indians. On the western bank of the Rio Grande, the settlers built their first town, San Gabriel. Their church went up in the Indian village. From this base, Oñate and some of his relatives led smaller expeditions to explore the area. One group traveled north and saw huge herds of buffalo. Another group, led by Oñate's nephew, came under attack when they sought out food from the Acoma Indians, and Oñate's nephew was killed.

Built on a mesa, the Acoma village was easily defended. One member of Oñate's settlement wrote, "There was a wall of large and small stones at the top, which they could roll down without showing themselves." However, Oñate was determined to punish the Acoma for killing his nephew. In January 1599, about 70 Spanish soldiers attacked the pueblo. In fierce fighting, the Spanish killed many Acoma warriors. One Spanish officer called for the Indians to surrender. One solder later said that the Acoma "replied that they wanted only to die, together with their women and children." The Acoma preferred death over Spanish punishment or rule.

After three days of fighting, the Spanish took control of the village. On Oñate's orders, almost all the survivors were forced into slavery, and the men also had a foot cut off. Oñate wanted the punishment to serve as a warning to other Pueblo: Do not resist Spanish rule. Yet Oñate knew his men were badly outnumbered, and he wrote to New Spain seeking more troops. In the meantime, he continued to explore the region, hoping to find silver and other minerals.

A Troubled Young Colony

During one of Oñate's expeditions, most of the settlers in San Gabriel left the village and returned to New Spain. They were tired of living in a remote area and struggling for food. Oñate sent one of his aides to New Spain and then Spain to recruit new settlers. The settlers who remained behind, including the missionaries, criticized how Oñate ran the colony. Officials in New Spain heard the complaints, and in 1607, King Philip III decided to replace Oñate with a new adelantado. Oñate resigned first, seeing that the colonists were "as exhausted, hard pressed, and in need of help as I am helpless to furnish it." Oñate lost 600,000 pesos of his own money while trying to start the New Mexico colony. That would be worth about $400,000 today.

The remaining colonists chose Oñate's son Cristóbal as the new governor. Soon, however, the king sent his own representative, Pedro de Peralta, to serve as governor. For a time, Philip had considered giving up on the New Mexico colony. News from the Franciscan monks changed his mind. The missionaries reported that 7,000 Indians had recently converted, and more were ready to become Christians. The numbers might have been false, but Philip accepted them and decided it was worth spending money in New Mexico for the sake of his religion.

When Peralta arrived in New Mexico in 1610, he found only a few settlers in San Gabriel. The rest had moved south along the Rio Grande, far from the pueblos. The spot had open space where the settlers could farm and graze their animals. They called their new town Santa Fe. Peralta moved to Santa Fe, making it the capital of New Mexico.

An early Spanish building made of adobe in Albuquerque, New Mexico, is shown in this hand-colored woodcut.

Peralta soon set out rules for how the colony would be run. Men and women in charge of households were named citizens, as were other males over 25 who were not servants or enslaved. The citizens voted for local officials who served as advisers to the governor. With these officials, the governor granted land to the citizens—the most respected men received the best land.

Life in Santa Fe

From the first days of the New Mexico colony, the settlers knew the importance of raising their own crops. The American Indians did not grow enough to feed themselves and the newcomers. The Spaniards often forced the Pueblo to prepare fields for crops and later raise the crops. Finding good farmland was hard, as the Indians owned the best land, and Spanish law prevented the settlers from stealing the land from them. Nevertheless, the available land was productive. In 1634, a missionary wrote, "This land . . . is the most . . . fertile of all the Indies . . . and produced an incredible quantity."

As in La Florida, the American Indians of the region that would one day be the U.S. Southwest raised corn, beans, and squash. The settlers introduced wheat, barley, and other European crops. They also brought in crops from New Spain, such as the chili pepper and the tomato. The Spaniards raised goats, sheep, cattle, and horses, and the animals became important both to the Pueblo and to tribes outside the region. The Apache, among others, raided New Mexican farms to steal the animals.

The Pueblo were key to the Spaniards' survival in New Mexico. They raised the food the settlers ate and wove the cloth used to make clothes. The Indians also introduced the settlers to deerskin clothing, which was more practical than the fancy clothing they had brought with them from Spain and New Spain. Under a system called *repartimiento,* the colonists were supposed to pay the Pueblo for the work they did in Spanish fields. Some settlers, however, refused to pay and forced the Indians to work long hours. Over time, the Pueblo began to resent the Spanish presence in their lands.

Missionaries in New Mexico

The missionary priests played an important role in the lives of both the American Indians and the settlers. The priests had the Indians build churches for the pueblos. These adobe buildings were fairly large, compared to the churches that the missionaries built in La Florida. The pueblo churches often had bell towers and other features found in European churches. The building style used at the missions, and later in California, was also

The Sheep of New Mexico

One of the most important things Spanish settlers took with them to New Mexico was the churro sheep. The male churro is known for having four horns, one large and one small on each side of his head. Churro grow enough wool that they can be sheared twice a year, and in colonial times, the sheep and their wool were a primary source of income for both settlers and American Indians. The Navajo in particular raised the churro for its wool. Their weavings from churro wool were highly valued. By the 1970s, the churro species had almost died out, but recent preservation efforts have increased the number of sheep. Today, the breed is officially known as the Navajo-churro.

used for other buildings, creating what is still called mission architecture. Even as new building styles have developed, this simple design is still used for some public buildings in the Southwest. The revival of mission architecture was strongest during the first few decades of the 20th century.

At the New Mexico missions, the priests lived with the Pueblo Indians, teaching them the Spanish language and the Roman Catholic faith. Some Indians believed that the priests were great shamans, since they brought new foods and tools with them. The priests at times tried to prevent the settlers from abusing the Indians. Treating them well was a better way to convince the Pueblo to accept Christianity. (The Spanish citizens, however, claimed that the missionaries often mistreated the Indians who worked for them.)

The local Indian shamans tried to convince the Pueblo to resist the missionaries and their teachings. In many cases, the Indians accepted some Catholic teachings while still following their traditional religions. The Spaniards knew little about these religions. The Pueblo did not talk about them and would not let strangers into their kivas, the special buildings where they held their religious ceremonies.

In the early days of Santa Fe, some missionaries struggled with the governor for power. At one point, the head priest kicked Peralta out of the Roman Catholic Church—a severe penalty among the deeply religious Spaniards. The feud ended and Peralta was allowed to rejoin the church, but the difficulties between church officials and governors continued for decades.

At the same time, the missionaries began to range far from the original Spanish settlements, seeking new converts. The first mission in the Estancia Valley, south of present-day Albuquerque, was built in 1613, and the Franciscans also roamed into Arizona and the lands of the Hopi Indians. This missionary work could be dangerous. The success of missions in the Estancia Valley drew the attention of some Apache, traditional foes of the Pueblo. Apache attacks forced the missions to close, and the Pueblo who lived in them moved to northern missions. Still, by 1632, the Franciscans in New Mexico had built 25 missions and said they had won 60,000 converts.

This ceremonial figure, painted on a kiva wall near the Rio Grande in New Mexico, probably dates from around 1500.

To officials in Spain, the missions were the only obvious sign that the colony of New Mexico was thriving. The settlers did not find minerals, and few Spaniards wanted to live there. By the 1660s, the Spanish population—including Africans, people of mixed ancestry, and American Indians who had adopted Spanish ways—was only about 2,500.

For the most part, the settlers were cut off from New Spain. The Franciscans ran the only regular supply line to the south, sending wagons and men on a round trip that took 18 months. The goods were also expensive, as the Spanish government taxed items sent into its colonies and limited what the settlers could make on their own. Except for a few wealthy families, the Spanish New Mexicans were poor. Still, they managed to survive. 🔲

New Contacts, New Troubles

6

As its colony in New Mexico slowly grew, Spain continued to expand its influence in La Florida. During the
early years of the 17th century, more Franciscans
arrived in St. Augustine and then set out for missions built
among the Guale Indians, reaching into what is now
Georgia. Mission work also continued with the Timucua to
the west and later with the Apalachee. The missionary
efforts there were hard, the Franciscans reported, because
the Apalachee were so far away and it was "impossible to
carry . . . provisions overland from . . . St. Augustine or to
assist [soldiers] or support them with what they need."

Native American chiefs sometimes visited St. Augustine
to demonstrate their loyalty to Spain to the officials there.
The chiefs were eager to trade for Spanish goods, and they
sometimes brought some of their people with them, to
leave behind as workers for the colonists. As in New Mexico,
Indians were forced to work for the missions. This hard
work, some historians suggest, made the Indians weak and
more likely die of disease. The American Indian population
continued to shrink because of the Spanish presence.

OPPOSITE This colored engraving depicts the Pueblo Revolt of 1680 in
New Mexico.

Rebellions in Florida

Armed conflict also reduced the Native American population in Florida. From the 1590s through the middle of the 17th century, each of the main American Indian groups rebelled against the Spanish. Each time, Spanish soldiers ended the violence.

In September 1597, the Guale attacked missions in Georgia. The rebellion was led by a chief's son, who had become angry when a mission priest refused to let him have more than one wife—a common custom among the Guale. The rebels killed almost all the Franciscans in the region and destroyed the missions. Father Luis de Oré later wrote about the attacks that "we encountered a great number of painted Indians, their faces smeared with red earth, and fitted out with bows and arrows. They seemed to be numberless and looked like demons."

The Spanish responded by sending 100 soldiers, along with 200 Christian Indians, to hunt down the rebels. Failing to find them, the troops burned villages and crops. For each of the next few years, the troops returned to destroy more villages. Finally, Guale chiefs decided to once again declare their loyalty to Spain. The chiefs eventually killed the rebels.

Fifty years later, the Apalachee rose up against the Spanish. Apalachee who had rejected Christianity joined with others who opposed the Spanish presence. The rebels killed several Spanish officials and Franciscans and burned seven of the missions in the region. A force of 31 Spanish soldiers and 500 Timucua warriors soon arrived to fight the rebels, who may have numbered in the thousands. After one long battle, both sides had heavy losses. The Spanish and their allies went back to St. Augustine. When a small force later returned to Apalachee lands, most of the rebels were ready to give up. They had not expected the Spanish to strike back so quickly and feared more losses. These rebels helped the Spanish capture the leaders of the revolt. The Spanish soon sent a large force of soldiers to live in the region.

By this time, the Apalachee were replacing the Timucua as the main suppliers of food and labor for the colonists. This meant that the Spanish gave more presents to Apalachee chiefs and fewer to the Timucua, angering the Timucua chiefs. In 1656, the Spanish feared an English attack in St. Augustine. The governor demanded that the Timucua and other tribes send soldiers to defend the town. A Timucua chief named Lúcas Menéndez refused, and he recruited other chiefs to start a rebellion.

This engraving shows Spanish soldiers battling American Indians in Florida in 1564. It was first published in Frankfurt, Germany, in 1591.

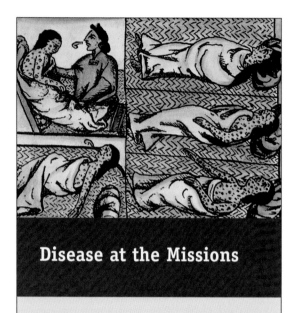

Disease at the Missions

As the Franciscans set up new missions, they spread disease to different parts of Florida. About half the Timucua living near missions built around 1615 died from some unknown epidemic. A more severe epidemic hit the St. Augustine region in 1655 and spread to the missions. Most likely smallpox, the epidemic killed perhaps half the Timucua and Guale in contact with the Spanish. The Apalachee were also affected by Spanish disease. Their population had been about 50,000 when Juan Ponce de León first came to Florida in 1513. By the middle of the 17th century, only about 10,000 Apalachee survived.

The Timucua killed seven people, including two African slaves. Some members of the tribe around St. Augustine refused to plant crops, meaning that the Spanish would not have food for the coming year. The rebels then withdrew and built a fort, knowing that the Spanish would come to punish them. Soldiers from both St. Augustine and the Apalachee, joined by other Indian allies, went to the fort. They convinced the rebels to surrender without a fight. The arrested rebels were either killed or taken prisoner.

Revolt in New Mexico

The Spanish faced an even more dangerous situation in New Mexico. By the end of the 1660s, the colony faced several problems. A severe drought had hit New Mexico, and the Pueblo could not grow enough food. Father Juan Bernal said in a report to Roman Catholic officials that "the whole land is at war with the very numerous . . . Apache Indians who kill all the Christian Indians they encounter . . . [and] for three years no crop has been harvested." Bernal noted that hundreds died of hunger while the Spanish settlers ate "the cowhides they have in their houses to sit on," but the settlers were running out of leather because their cattle were dying.

In the middle of these terrible times, some Pueblo thought that the tribes should return to their old religions. In 1670, the Spanish prevented a planned rebellion. In the arrested leader's home they found tribal religious items. During the next decade, as illness added to the tribes' troubles, more Pueblo began to seek comfort in their traditional faith.

Spanish officials tried to cut off the growing power of the shamans who still practiced the old beliefs. In 1675, Governor Juan Francisco Treviño sent soldiers into the pueblos to arrest almost 50 tribal priests. Most were whipped, while three were executed. Armed Indians forced the release of the punished shamans. One of the shamans was a man known as Popé. Like many Pueblo, he was tired of Spanish rule and the restrictions against practicing the old religion. After his arrest and punishment, Popé began planning a rebellion against the colonists. He called on all the pueblos to unite and wage a war for freedom.

On August 9, 1680, Popé and his supporters began their attacks, and the major fighting took place the next day. The united Pueblo forces and some Apache allies easily outnumbered the Spanish. The Indians drove off the settlers' livestock, burned their churches, and took horses, guns, swords, and other belongings from the defeated colonists. Almost all the pueblos took part, and the Zuni and Hopi farther west also rebelled.

> **Fast Fact**
>
> The Pueblo Revolt of 1680 marked the only time that Spain lost part of its empire to American Indians whom it had previously conquered.

After destroying settlements in the north, the rebels marched to Santa Fe. Settlers had flocked there and to the Spanish settlement at Isleta. In Santa Fe, Governor Antonio de Otermín saw the rebels preparing to attack the colonists. One report said that the Indians, "having killed as many of the settlers elsewhere as possible, now danced in their glee around the . . . refugees who had taken safety in the government buildings."

On August 15, a rebel leader offered Otermín a choice. He could fight the rebel force of several thousand with just his 100 or so soldiers, or he could take the settlers out of New Mexico. Otermín refused to leave, and several days later, his men rushed out of the government buildings to attack the Pueblo. The Spanish managed to kill several hundred Indians while suffering only a few losses before returning to safety. Still, the Pueblo had several advantages. They still outnumbered the Spanish, and the settlers were running out of food and water. Finally, on August 21, Otermín led the settlers out of Santa Fe to the west Texas town of El Paso. The Pueblo threatened them, but did not attack. They just wanted the Spanish to leave.

Planning to Return

In the fall of 1681, Otermín tried to take back the abandoned colony but failed. In El Paso, many settlers lost hope that they would ever return to the Rio Grande valley. Some returned to New Spain. Those who remained faced attacks from nearby

Indians. At times, the Spanish considered leaving El Paso, but some officials did not want to give up on the colony in New Mexico. Likewise, the Franciscans did not want to abandon the converts they had made among the Indians.

In 1691, Diego de Vargas took over as governor for the settlers in El Paso. He was a soldier with experience battling Native Americans, and he led the fight to regain northern New Mexico. He led about 200 troops north to take on the Pueblo in 1692.

Vargas knew he was outnumbered, but he hoped his bold manner and generous terms would convince the Pueblo to surrender. At several pueblos, he had his men say prayers, rather than fire their guns. Vargas then announced that the Indians would be forgiven for their rebellion if they accepted Spanish rule. Surprisingly, most agreed. Even in Santa Fe, the Indians did not attack. By this time, Popé was dead, and the Pueblo were no longer united, which may have influenced their decision to accept Vargas's demands.

Vargas returned to El Paso a hero. One official wrote that thanks to Vargas, "an entire realm was restored to the Majesty of our lord and king . . . without wasting a single ounce of

Diego de Vargas

Diego de Vargas (unknown–1704) came from a noble family, and he had often proved his bravery. Once, while serving as a government official in New Spain, he had dashed into a burning church to save some of the sacred objects inside. After he regained New Mexico, Vargas tried not to upset the Pueblo. Unlike other Spanish officials, he did not destroy the Pueblo kivas. He also dealt fairly with his Indian allies. In 1697, however, Vargas ran into trouble with Spanish officials. He refused to give up his post as governor of New Mexico and was thrown into jail for five months. A few years later, Vargas was able to win back his honor and briefly served as governor again.

[gun]powder, unsheathing a sword, or . . . without costing the Royal Treasury a single [coin]."

The next year, some of the original settlers moved back into the Rio Grande valley. Other settlers were recruited from New Spain. As the settlers arrived, some of the Pueblo went back on their word to obey the Spanish. For several years, Vargas battled the Indians who did not accept his control. Finally, by the end of the 1690s, Spain once again ruled the people and lands of New Mexico's Rio Grande valley.

Missions to the West

During the difficult years in the Rio Grande valley, Spain was extending its influence farther west. Eusebio Kino, a Jesuit priest originally from Italy, led the Spanish efforts to convert American Indians in what is now southern Arizona. He arrived in Mexico shortly after the Pueblo Revolt of 1680. Jesuits had already served in La Florida, but Kino was among the first of his order to go to the region that would later be the U.S. Southwest.

Kino began his missionary work in Baja (Lower) California before being sent to Sonora, New Spain, in 1687. From there, he went north into Arizona, where he converted the Pima Indians. Like other Jesuits, Kino was often called "the Black Robe," referring to the clothing the members of his order wore. On several trips into Arizona, Kino founded missions as far north as modern-day Phoenix.

Fast Fact

In 1692, Father Kino reached a spot called Bac, in the land of the Tohono O'odham Indians, not far from Tucson. The mission there, San Xavier del Bac, is the only surviving mission from Kino's time.

He introduced cattle and other livestock to the tribes of the region and taught them new methods of farming.

Kino was also an explorer. In between founding missions, he traveled across the deserts of the present-day U.S. Southwest and sailed on many of its major rivers. He was the first European to see many of the sites of the desert and the first to reach the Pacific Ocean by an overland route. At the time, the Spanish thought Baja California was an island. Kino's travels proved that it was a peninsula. On his expeditions, Kino made maps that were used in Europe for many years.

Kino's efforts did not lead to another successful Spanish settlement. Few mission priests served in Arizona, and Kino could not convince the crown to start missions in Alta (Upper) California. Still, the Jesuit did introduce Spanish farming methods, Catholic teachings, and the Spanish language to this part of the Southwest. ▣

International Conflicts

7

When Spain first launched its colonies in La Florida and New Mexico, it was the only European power with a permanent presence in what became the United States. Yet through the 17th century, a number of other European nations built colonies in North America. France created New France, which is today the Canadian province of Quebec. From there, French traders and missionaries headed south into the Great Lakes region. For a time, Sweden and the Netherlands had small colonies along the Hudson and Delaware Rivers. England, which became part of Great Britain after 1707, started colonies in Massachusetts and Virginia, eventually sending colonists up and down the Atlantic coast. By the 1680s, the English and the French were Spain's major rivals in the New World.

The silver mines of Peru and New Spain produced great wealth. However, Spanish kings spent huge amounts of money running other New World colonies, such as Florida and New Mexico, that were not as successful. Spain's empire also included the Philippines in Asia and European regions

OPPOSITE The expedition of René-Robert Cavelier, Sieur de La Salle, is shown landing in Texas in 1685. The Spanish were alarmed at the French presence in Texas, so close to New Spain.

such as Italy and the Spanish Netherlands. Since France and Great Britain also wanted to trade overseas and expand their empires, they often came into conflict with Spain. Running an empire and fighting wars were expensive. In 1640, one Spanish official wrote that Spain could have dominated the world if it had spent less on war. By the 1680s, Spain saw itself coming under growing threats in North America.

The French Reach Texas

In 1682, René-Robert Cavelier, Sieur de La Salle, led a French expedition down the Mississippi River from present-day Canada. When La Salle reached the mouth of the Mississippi, he claimed the land there for France. He named it Louisiana, in honor of the French king, Louis XIV. Two years later, La Salle sailed from France with settlers, hoping to start a colony in Louisiana.

The settlers missed their planned landing spot, near the mouth of the Mississippi, and ended up in Spanish lands. They came ashore early in 1685 near present-day Corpus Christi, Texas. La Salle soon realized he was not in Louisiana. He claimed the land for France and built a fort, but illness, American Indian attacks, and lack of food doomed the colony. La Salle died in Texas in 1687, and some survivors headed north to Canada.

When officials in New Spain learned about the French settlement, they wrote to Spain, calling for fast action to "pluck out the thorn that has been thrust into America's heart." The French presence alarmed the Spanish, who did not want their rivals so close to New Spain. They sent land

and sea expeditions to find the French and force them out. By the time they finally found the French settlement in 1689, it was abandoned.

Spanish officials still worried that the French would return to eastern Texas. To strengthen their claim to the land, Spain began to send its first missionaries into the region. In 1690, the first mission church in eastern Texas was built near modern-day Augusta. Staffed by only three priests and three soldiers, the mission soon failed, as hostile Hisinais Indians threatened the Spanish. The mission closed in 1693.

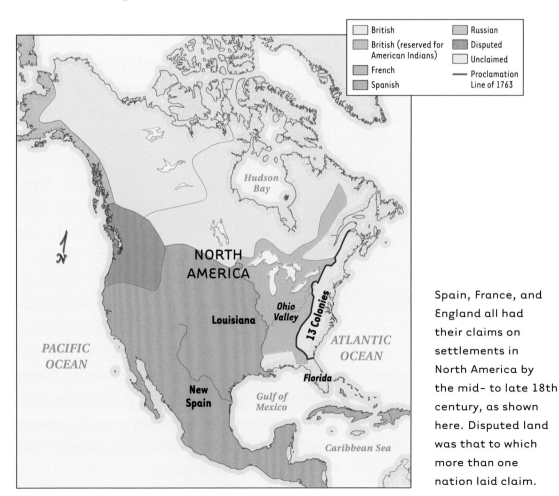

Spain, France, and England all had their claims on settlements in North America by the mid- to late 18th century, as shown here. Disputed land was that to which more than one nation laid claim.

New Protection

The arrival of the English in South Carolina led officials in St. Augustine to take action to protect themselves from possible English attacks. In 1672, construction began on the Castillo de San Marcos, a huge stone fort. The building looked like a large square with an arrow-shaped point coming off each corner. The fort's walls were 26 feet (8 m) high and later extended another 7 feet (2 m). The stone blocks came from a nearby island and were sent by raft to St. Augustine. Hundreds of converted Indians worked to build the fort. The Castillo de San Marcos was completed in 1692. The fort still stands in St. Augustine.

Starting in 1699, the French began building successful colonies along the coast, in present-day Mississippi and Alabama. By this time, the Spanish had built a fort in Pensacola, Florida, to prevent the French from moving eastward along the gulf. In 1715, the Spanish began building a string of missions in eastern Texas, a sign of their plan to create a permanent presence there.

Threat from the Carolinas

In 1670, English settlers from the West Indian island of Barbados founded the colony of Charles Town (later Charleston) in South Carolina. Unlike the Spanish, the English were not as concerned about converting American Indians to Christianity. Like the French, the Carolinians were willing to trade guns to the tribes they met.

The English encouraged the Indians to raid the villages of tribes friendly to Spain and take their captives as slaves. Starting in 1680, the English and their Indian allies also attacked Spanish missions in Georgia. By 1685, the enemy raids had forced Spain to close its missions in Georgia, and Florida faced a growing threat of attack.

Tensions between the Charles Town settlers and the Spanish grew over the issue of slavery. The English relied heavily on slave labor to raise their crops. Slaves who escaped from the English settlement and managed to reach Florida were warmly welcomed by the Spanish in St. Augustine as workers in the colony. In 1693, King Charles II of Spain officially approved a policy to let escaped slaves gain their freedom in Florida, angering the English in the Carolinas.

In addition, the English and Spanish disliked each other's religions, since the English were Protestants. The English also hoped to someday expand their colony southward into lands that Spain claimed. In 1702, South Carolina governor James Moore launched a raid on Spanish Florida with 1,500 attackers. St. Augustine, with a total population of about the same number, had only about 300 soldiers to defend it. The whole town fled to the fort of Castillo de San Marcos. The invading English destroyed the town, but they could not take over the fort. They fled when the troops from Cuba arrived.

In the years to come, the Carolina colonists and their Indian allies continued to raid Florida. Their attacks forced more missions to close. In 1710, an English writer noted that outside St. Augustine, "there remains not now so much as one village with ten houses in it, in all Florida that is subject to the Spaniards." The number of Spanish

Fast Fact

The 1702 invasion of Florida was part of a larger conflict called the War of the Spanish Succession (1701–1714). England and its allies wanted to prevent France from placing a new king who was related to France's King Louis XIV on the Spanish throne. In the Americas, the war was called Queen Anne's War, named for England's ruler during most of the war.

settlers and missionaries continued to fall. By the middle of the 18th century, only 10 Spanish monks remained in the colony.

The non-Spanish population in St. Augustine grew. American Indians seeking to avoid raiding tribes sometimes sought protection there, as did slaves from the Carolinas. After 1738, the slaves often went to Fort Mose. Former slaves from the Carolinas built this fort and a nearby town just north of St. Augustine. Yet few Spanish settlers wanted to live in La Florida, fearing more English and Indian raids.

A Weakening Empire

The War of the Spanish Succession ended in 1714. King Louis XIV achieved his goal of making one of his relatives— his grandson Philip—the king of Spain. When the war ended, Philip V strengthened his military. Still, Spain's navy could not compete with Great Britain's, and some Spaniards thought the crown had not done enough to make money in the Americas.

Especially in North America, it was clear that the Spanish presence was weak. Spanish settlers in Pensacola and St. Augustine could not count on Spanish merchants in New Spain or the West Indies to supply them with goods. They had to trade with more successful English and French settlements to survive. In addition to the troubles in Florida, the Spanish also struggled to expand in the present-day U.S. Southwest. Officials in New Mexico still wanted to start missions in Texas. The most successful was at San Antonio,

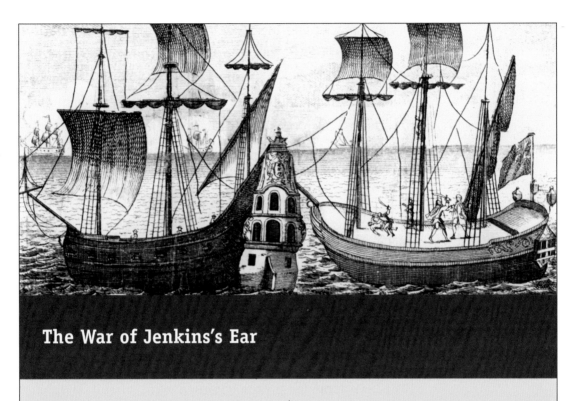

The War of Jenkins's Ear

During the 1730s, tensions between Great Britain and Spain spread to the oceans. In 1731, a Spanish sailor cut off the ear of a British sea captain who had been raiding Spanish ships. Some people in Great Britain demanded that Spain be punished for this action, and war broke out between the two nations. In the War of Jenkins's Ear, which began in 1739, much of the fighting took place in Georgia. The first British settlers had reached that colony in 1733. In 1740, Governor James Oglethorpe led an army of settlers and American Indians against the Spanish in St. Augustine. Once again, the Spanish retreated into the Castillo de San Marcos for protection and held off the British assault. Two years later, Spanish troops from Florida invaded Georgia but were driven back. Oglethorpe tried another attack on St. Augustine in 1743, but that also failed. By this time, Great Britain and Spain were on opposite sides in a European conflict known as the War of the Austrian Succession (1740–1748). The fighting finally ended in 1748.

which was founded in 1718. Other missions, however, faced attacks from Great Plains Indians, such as the Comanche, Wichita, and Apache. The arrival of guns and horses had made these tribes difficult foes. After one raid, a military officer said, "The enemy [is] so superior . . . in firearms as well as number that our destruction seems probable."

Spanish Louisiana

Spain did not challenge France when it established New Orleans in 1718, about 100 miles (160 km) north of the mouth of the Mississippi River. After years of struggle, the colony of New Orleans began to grow, and French trade grew farther north along the Mississippi River.

In 1754, fighting broke out between the French and British in land they both claimed west of the Allegheny Mountains. Each side had Indian allies, and in North America, the conflict was called the French and Indian War (1754–1763). The war also involved other European nations and was fought on several continents.

In 1761, Spain's King Charles III signed a treaty with France. He agreed to help France fight the British. Within two years, the British and their allies had won the war. Spain was forced to give Florida to the British. Partly to make up for Spain's loss there, France gave Spain its Louisiana colony. France could not afford to run the colony, and Spain wanted it as a buffer between the growing British colonies in North America and New Spain.

The land that Spain received from France stretched from the Gulf of Mexico into Canada. Spain now controlled the entire west bank of the Mississippi River, as well as the city of New Orleans. In 1766, the first Spanish governor arrived. He faced angry French colonists who were upset to be under Spanish rule.

The French residents grew increasingly angry as Spain tried to clamp down on smuggling and limit their trade with French colonies in the West Indies. In 1768, some of the business owners of New Orleans organized a rebellion. They forced the Spanish to leave the colony. The next year, a large Spanish force sailed from Cuba to regain control of Louisiana. General Alejandro O'Reilly met with the rebels, and they surrendered rather than fight. The leaders were later executed.

While in Louisiana, O'Reilly replaced most of the old French laws with Spanish laws. Under Spanish rule, the colonists could no longer enslave American Indians. The enslavement of Africans, however, was still allowed. In a reference to how casual frontier life could be, O'Reilly wrote, "Having been informed . . . that, during divine worship, the church is filled with dogs, I request the commandant to prevent the repetition of this breach of decency."

O'Reilly remained in control until 1770, when he turned the government over to a civilian governor, Luis de Unzaga y Amezaga. In general, the French residents of Louisiana welcomed Unzaga's rule. He won some support when he married a French woman, and he made merchants happy by encouraging trade with the British and their colonies in America. Unzaga served as governor until 1777.

Into California

8

With the loss of Florida in 1763, Spain paid new attention to the west coast of North America. For several decades, Russian explorers and traders had sailed along the coast, meeting with the Native Americans who lived in Alaska. One Russian official suggested that his country could "extend its possessions as far as California and Mexico." Spain saw Russia as a new rival in lands it had claimed for centuries. Adding to the threat were British and Dutch ships that sailed off the coast of California, waiting to attack Spanish vessels.

By the 1760s, Spain had a growing presence in Baja California. Missions founded decades before were strengthened by José Gálvez, the inspector-general of New Spain. Gálvez was ordered to increase the amount of money New Spain sent to the Spanish crown. He also wanted to extend Spanish influence north into Alta California to keep out the Russians and other European rivals. In 1768, Gálvez began planning an expedition into what is now the state of California.

The year before, King Charles III had told the Jesuits to leave their missions in New Spain. The Jesuits had made

OPPOSITE Spanish missionary priests were among the first Europeans to settle in California. Like the missionary in this engraving from about 1900, their goal was to convert the Indians to Christianity.

many enemies by amassing wealth and power and by asserting the church's authority over kings and other political figures. Charles sent the Franciscans to take over the Jesuit missions in Baja California. One of the priests who arrived was Junípero Serra. Gálvez chose him to found the first missions in Alta California.

Travels through California

To lead the trip to California, called "the Sacred Expedition," Gálvez chose Gaspar de Portolá. Early in 1769, two ships left Baja California for San Diego. Portolá and Serra were in one of two groups that traveled by land and met the ships there. Serra, who had an infected leg, could not walk and had to be lifted onto a mule. He wrote, "Even though I should die on the way, I shall not turn back." The land groups brought with them cattle and horses, and the Spaniards carried seeds so they could plant crops at their new missions.

By July 1, the soldiers, sailors, and priests had reunited in San Diego. Of the roughly 300 who left Baja California on the Sacred Expedition, one-third had died from sickness along the way. Instead of continuing on, as he had originally planned, Serra stayed in San Diego, and within a few weeks, he had founded the first California mission. Meanwhile, Portolá and other members of the expedition headed north, hoping to reach Monterey. The Spanish explorer Sebastián Vizcaíno

> **Fast Fact**
>
> Gaspar de Portolá was the governor of Baja California, as well as the leader of the Sacred Expedition. After the expedition, he returned to New Spain and never went back to California.

had anchored in the harbor there more than 150 years before.

Portolá and his small band left San Diego on July 14. They traveled close to the coast. The American Indians they met were friendly and often brought generous amounts of food to the explorers. The expedition reached Monterey at the end of September, but Portolá did not see the harbor Vizcaíno had described. Continuing farther north, Portolá and his men came to what is now called San Francisco Bay. Portolá was disappointed he had not found Monterey Bay, as he had been ordered to do. With the expedition running out of food, Portolá decided to return to San Diego.

Conditions were not much better there. At first, the Ipai and neighboring Tipai had been friendly to the Spanish. As illness killed some of the soldiers, the Indians became bold and began stealing from the Spanish. After one brief battle, the soldiers built a simple fort, called a presidio. In the years to come, the Spanish would build presidios along the coast to protect the priests working in the missions.

Junípero Serra

Junípero Serra (1713–1784) was born on the Spanish island of Mallorca. As a teen, he studied with the Franciscans and joined the order in 1730. By the age of 24, he was a respected professor, but he decided to become a missionary. In 1749, he left Spain for New Spain. His parents were sad to seem him go. Serra wrote in a letter before he left, "We must allow nothing in this life to cause us sadness. Our clear duty is to conform ourselves in every way to the will of God so as to prepare well for death. Nothing else really matters."

In New Spain, Serra worked tirelessly to convert the Indians. He was named head of the missions in Baja California after the Jesuits were asked to leave. After going to Alta California in 1769, Serra remained there the rest of his life. In recent years, some Roman Catholics have worked to have Serra named a saint in that church.

The Spanish settle-
ment of San
Francisco, shown
here, remained small
for years after its
founding in 1776.

With supplies almost gone, Portolá planned for the entire expedition to return to Baja California. Serra did not want to leave. He feared that the missionary effort in California would end if the expedition failed. Finally, in March 1770, a supply ship arrived. After a large feast, Portolá prepared to head north again in search of Monterey Bay. Serra also made the journey. When the expedition finally found Monterey, he held a mass at the site that became the second California mission, San Carlos Borroméo. A second presidio was built in Monterey, which became the capital of Alta California.

American Indians and Colonists

Over the next two years, Serra and the other Franciscans built three more missions between Monterey and San Diego. Serra was determined to make Christians out of California's Indians. Some came to the missions on their own, curious to learn more about the newcomers. Others were forced into the missions by Spanish soldiers, and once they converted, the Indians could not leave. Serra and the Franciscans called the Indians *gente sin razón*—"people without reason," or intelligence. The Spaniards called themselves *gente de razón,* or "people of reason." This attitude explained why Serra thought he knew what was best for the Indians.

Just as in New Mexico and La Florida, the Christian Indians had to work for the missionaries. The Indians raised crops, took care of livestock, and made such everyday items as candles, soap, bricks, and shoes. Inside the missions, men and women slept in separate buildings, so husbands and wives were kept apart. European diseases spread among the Indians, and the Spanish sometime beat Christian Indians who disobeyed mission rules. Serra and the other priests thought they were doing the Indians a favor by teaching them Christianity and Spanish farming methods. The Indians, however, lost their traditional way of life and their freedom. As one Franciscan later said, "They live well free but as soon as we reduce them to a Christian and community life . . . they fatten, sicken, and die."

By 1774, fewer than 200 Spanish colonists lived in California. The colony was far from the trading centers of New Spain, and the Spanish government refused to let the colonists trade with other nations. To help California grow, the viceroy of New Spain, Antonio María de Bucareli, sponsored an expedition to find a land route from Sonora to California.

In January 1774, Juan Bautista de Anza led the expedition that successfully found a route from Arizona to San

Before Portolá and Serra

Although the Spanish did not settle Alta California until 1769, they had explored its coast for centuries. In 1542, Juan Rodríguez Cabrillo sailed from New Spain to the harbor later named San Diego Bay. Continuing his voyage north along the coast of Alta California, he came ashore several times. Several decades later, large ships sailing from Spain's colony in the Philippines passed along the California coast on their way to New Spain. Sebastián Vizcaíno's expedition of 1602 and 1603 marked the last major Spanish exploration of Alta California. He and his three ships visited many of the places Cabrillo had seen. Vizcaíno gave many of these sites names that are still used today, such as San Diego, Santa Barbara, Monterey, and Carmel.

Gabriel, a mission not far from present-day Los Angeles. The next year, after returning to Arizona, Anza led a group of 240 settlers—mostly women and children—and 1,000 animals into California. They reached San Gabriel in January 1776, doubling the Spanish presence in California.

By the time Anza reached San Gabriel in 1776, the missions were facing severe threats from the American Indian tribes. The missionaries had converted 2,000 Indians, but many more remained outside the missions and disliked the Spanish presence. At San Gabriel, Anza received a message to come to San Diego. The previous November, non-Christian Ipai and Tipai Indians had united with some converts to burn the mission there. The situation was still tense when Anza arrived and asserted Spanish control. Father Serra asked that the leaders of the revolt not be killed so he could convert them.

Anza and the settlers he had led into California then headed north to Monterey. They explored the area around San Francisco Bay, but Anza returned to Arizona before the settlers built their presidio. The Franciscans also built a mission. San Francisco remained the most northerly Spanish settlement in California for more than 40 years.

Although missionaries and soldiers controlled the first Spanish settlements in California, the situation soon changed. In 1777, Felipe de Neve became governor of California. He decided to create civilian villages, or pueblos, that would be separate from the missions. The first one, San Jose, was founded in 1777. The second was Nuestra Señora la Reina de los Angeles de Porciúncula, founded two years later. Today, that settlement is better known as Los Angeles, California's largest city and the second-largest in the United States.

American Indians are shown attending a mass for the dead at a California mission.

The colony of California grew slowly. Sea travel from New Spain was expensive, and trouble with the Quechan Indians led Spanish officials to stop using the land route between Arizona and California. Only the children of the first Spanish settlers helped the colony grow, and only the money paid to soldiers stationed at the presidios kept the economy alive. California, like New Mexico and La Florida, was almost a forgotten part of the Spanish empire.

The Spanish World after the American Revolution

By the time San Francisco was founded, the continent of North America was once again the scene of war. To the east and north of Spain's lands in Louisiana, the 13 British colonies had just declared their independence. With this act, they created the United States. In 1777, U.S. officials asked Spain for aid in their war against Great Britain. King Charles III refused, though Spain secretly gave some money so the United States could buy supplies. Finally, in 1779, Spain declared war on Great Britain, though it did not send troops to fight in North America.

After the war, the United States gained its independence and Spain regained Florida from Great Britain. The United States now also claimed lands up to the east bank of the Mississippi. The other side, Spanish Louisiana, was mostly an unexplored region, with few Europeans living there. The main Spanish presence north of New Spain was in New Orleans, Santa Fe, San Antonio, and scattered settlements in the present-day U.S. Southwest and California.

To many U.S. citizens, the Spanish lands around them seemed a natural part of their country. In the decades to come, the United States gained those territories. Through the Louisiana Purchase in 1803, President Thomas Jefferson added New Orleans and a major part of the Spanish lands west of the Mississippi to the United States. In 1818, U.S. troops entered East (Spanish) Florida. The next year, Spain gave up all its claims to Florida. Soon after, Mexico won its independence from Spain. It could not stop the U.S. drive to expand in the West. After the Mexican-American War (1846–1848), the United States took possession of California and New Mexico.

Some U.S. citizens came into these Spanish-speaking lands convinced that they were better than the people they conquered. Some U.S. residents disliked the religion of the Mexican Americans and their lack of democratic traditions. U.S. businesses often gave Mexican Americans the worst jobs and used legal trickery to take their lands.

Despite the prejudice they faced, Mexican Americans stayed in the United States. These original Mexican Americans were joined by immigrants from Central and South America. Together, the native Spanish-speaking population and the immigrants created the Latino culture that thrives today.

Although Spain lost control of its empire north of Mexico, the Spanish influence remains. Spanish settlers introduced their language, architecture, livestock, and Roman Catholic faith. Today's Latino Americans can trace their culture in the United States to the efforts of conquistadores, priests, and settlers who came centuries before them.

Timeline

1492	Christopher Columbus founds the first Spanish colony in the New World, on the island of Hispaniola.
1513	Juan Ponce de León explores Florida.
1528	Pánfilo de Narváez leads an expedition to Florida.
1539	Hernando de Soto leads a three-year expedition into what is now the southeastern United States and across the Mississippi River. Marcos de Niza and Esteban explore New Mexico.
1540	Francisco Vásquez de Coronado leads an expedition into New Mexico and eventually goes as far north as Kansas.
1562	The French start a settlement in Florida—land claimed by Spain.
1565	Pedro Menéndez de Avilés goes to Florida to drive out the French. He founds St. Augustine.
1582	Antonio de Espejo explores parts of Arizona, Texas, and New Mexico.
1598	Juan Oñate leads settlers into New Mexico.
1602–1603	Sebastián Vizcaíno explores California.
1680	Popé leads a successful Pueblo revolt against Spanish rule.
1692	Diego de Vargas leads the reconquest of New Mexico; Eusebio Kino starts a mission near modern-day Tucson, Arizona.
1718	The mission at San Antonio, Texas, is founded.
1763	After the French and Indian War, Spain receives Louisiana from France, but loses Florida to Great Britain.
1769	Junípero Serra and Gaspar de Portolá lead an expedition into California. Serra founds the first California mission at San Diego.
1776	Juan Bautista de Anza leads settlers from Arizona to California and helps end an American Indian rebellion at San Diego.
1779	Los Angeles is founded as California's second civilian settlement.

Glossary

adobe Building material made out of dried mud and straw.

archaeologists Scientists who study ancient people by finding and examining the items they left behind.

civilizations Societies found in particular times and places with high levels of politics and arts.

criollos Settlers born in Latin America to Spanish parents.

domesticate To change a wild plant or animal over time so it can be used by humans.

encomienda A system under which American Indians granted their labor to the Spanish and paid them tribute, in return for which the Spanish were responsible for protecting and converting the Indians.

kivas Underground rooms built by Pueblos for holding their ceremonies.

mesa A high, flat area of land found in deserts.

mestizo A person with both Spanish and American Indian ancestry.

New Spain Mexico, the present-day U.S. Southwest, and Central America.

presidio A fort and garrison.

pueblo A town.

repartimiento A law requiring American Indians to work Spanish lands; the Indians were supposed to be paid but often were not.

shaman An American Indian medicine man.

viceroy The governor of New Spain.

Further Reading

Books

Blitz, John H., and Jason Baird Jackson, eds. *Indians of the Southeast.* Peterborough, NH: Cobblestone, 2003.

Broida, Marian. *The Pueblo.* New York: Marshall Cavendish Benchmark, 2006.

McIntosh, Kenneth. *First Encounters between Spain and the Americas: Two Worlds Meet.* Philadelphia: Mason Crest, 2006.

Thompson, Linda. *The Spanish in America.* Vero Beach, FL: Rourke, 2006.

Williams, Jack S. *Indians of the California Mission Frontier.* New York: PowerKids Press, 2004.

Worth, Richard. *Ponce de León and the Age of Spanish Exploration in World History.* Berkeley Heights, NJ: Enslow, 2003.

Web Sites

Florida Then & Now: A Short History of Florida, http://fcit.usf.edu/florida/lessons/ lessons.htm

History of the Spanish Empire, http://www.historyworld. net/wrldhis/PlainTextHistories.asp? groupid=1734&HistoryID=ab49

Spanish History in Santa Fe, http://www.santafe.com/ history/spanish_history.html

National Museum of the American Indian, http://www.nmai.si.edu/

Bibliography

Books

Elliott, J.H. *Imperial Spain, 1469–1716.* London: Penguin, 2002.

Galgano, Robert C. *Feast of Souls: Indians and Spaniards in the Seventeenth-Century Missions of Florida and New Mexico.* Albuquerque: University of New Mexico Press, 2005.

Kessell, John L. *Spain in the Southwest: A Narrative History of Colonial New Mexico, Arizona, Texas, and California.* Norman, OK: University of Oklahoma Press, 2002.

Kukla, Jon. *A Wilderness So Immense: The Louisiana Purchase and the Destiny of America.* New York: Alfred A. Knopf, 2003.

Lightfoot, Kent. *Indians, Missionaries, and Merchants: The Legacy of Colonial Encounters on the California Frontiers.* Berkeley: University of California Press, 2005.

Mann, Charles C. *1491: New Revelations of the Americas before Columbus.* New York: Alfred A. Knopf, 2005.

Web Sites

National Geographic News. "Americas Settled by Two Groups of Early Humans, Study Says." URL: http://news.nationalgeographic.com/news/2005/12/1212_051212_humans_americas.html. Downloaded on June 6, 2006.

PBS. "New Perspectives on THE WEST: Archives of THE WEST." URL: http://www.pbs.org/weta/thewest/resources/archives/. Downloaded on June 6, 2006.

Index

About the Author

Michael Burgan

Michael Burgan holds a B.A. in history, with an emphasis in American studies, from the University of Connecticut. He completed one year of graduate studies in writing, publishing, and literature at Emerson College. Burgan was a senior writer at Weekly Reader Corporation. He is currently a freelance writer. In 22 years, he has authored 18 books for children and young adults, as well as a large number of articles for the *New York Times, Sports Illustrated Kids, National Geographic World,* and the *Hartford Advocate.*

Mark Overmyer-Velázquez

Mark Overmyer-Velázquez, general editor and author of the preface included in each of the volumes, holds a BA in History and German Literature from the University of British Columbia, and MA, MPhil and PhDs in Latin American and Latino History from Yale University. While working on a new book project on the history of Mexican migration to the United States, he teaches undergraduate and graduate courses in Latin American and U.S. Latina/o history at the University of Connecticut.